REEL MAGICIANS

The Art and Science of Magic in Hollywood Movies

GLEN WEISSENBERGER

THE WEISSENBERGER POPULAR CULTURE SERIES

Published in the United States by
Eclectus Press, LLC
River Forest, Illinois

ISBN-13: 9780996757171
ISBN-10: 0996757171

www.weissenbergerartisticalliance.com

TABLE OF CONTENTS

INTRODUCTION

The most beautiful experience we can have is the mysterious.
It is the fundamental emotion that stands
at the cradle of true art and true science.
Whoever does not know it and can no longer wonder,
no longer marvel, is as good as dead, and his eyes are dimmed.

ALBERT EINSTEIN

A NYONE who has ever been a member of a magic organization, such as the International Brotherhood of Magicians, or the Society of American Magicians, knows that individuals who are attracted to the performance of magic and its allied arts come from extremely diverse backgrounds. Among both hobbyists and professionals, there is no stereotypical magician. Even though magic itself may be categorized in distinct ways, such as "close-up," "parlor," and "stage," those who practice in each of these arenas are all quite different.

Although each magician is unique, all share an appreciation of mystery and its ability to provide wonder and delight. Magicians have a common understanding that a world in which everything is known and understood simply cannot exist. This inability to comprehend everything in a worldly order can lead to frustration and discomfort—or it can be a source of marvel and inspiration. When magic is expertly and artistically performed, the magician shows us good reason not to be perturbed, but to be delighted by the world's mystery.

Moreover, when a magician is portrayed in a movie, we are not only able to see the magic they perform, but we are also given the ability to peer into their human persona. Depending on the film, we might be afforded a small, intriguing glimpse into their real character, or we may be allowed an intricate exploration of their psyche. Films about magicians, therefore, provide a unique opportunity to see not only dazzling feats of magic, but also to develop a better understanding of what would motivate one to learn its art and science.

Any book discussing magicians and the movies would be remiss if it did not point out the fact that it is no coincidence that the "golden age" of modern magic burgeoned concurrently with the "Golden Age of Hollywood." As chronicled in both Eric Barnouw's *The Magician and the Cinema* (1981) and Matthew Solomon's *Disappearing Tricks: Silent Film, Houdini, and the New Magic of the Twentieth Century* (2010), stage magicians were among the first film performers, filmmakers, and film exhibitors. By incorporating their performances into moving pictures, magicians no longer catered only to the upper echelons of society with the means to enjoy live performances. The combination of the new cinema with classical theatrical magic drew a much broader audience in the early twentieth century then conjuring alone had ever attracted before. Consequently, the growth of the motion picture industry had an important role in cultivating the audiences of the likes of Houdini, Thurston, Keller, and Blackstone.

The confluence and then divergence of film and theatrical magic is a fascinating story, and the mystery that magic and movies share illuminates how these two forms of entertainment first complemented one another, but then ultimately came to compete with one another. The lengthy bibliographies in both the Solomon and the Barnouw books are testaments to the enduring fascination with the intertwined history of contemporary film and modern conjuring.

This book, however, makes no pretense of being a work that contributes to the scholarship on film and magic. Rather, it is offered as a guide to anyone who enjoys both forms of entertainment and seeks insight into whether a particular movie might be a rewarding experience for the interests, taste, and age of the viewer.

To accomplish its modest objectives, this book provides a discussion of twenty-six films in which magicians play important roles. Specific criteria were used to select films in which the magician is a character. Notably excluded are films—many quite excellent—that depict magicians as having supernatural powers. For inclusion herein, the magic performed in the movie must, at least theoretically, be capable of execution without violating the laws of physics.

Also, included in this book is a featured bonus chapter: Woody Allen, who has written and directed several movies about magicians, also wrote a play, *The Floating Light Bulb*, which was performed on Broadway in the summer of 1981. The play, which meets the criteria used for selecting films in this book, is a unique piece of theater featuring magic effects performed by the central character. Because this book includes reviews of Mr. Allen's films about magicians, it seemed only appropriate to include a discussion of this remarkable play.

These criteria are important to the goals of the book, which are to provide insight into the worldly mortals who create the illusion of possessing unworldly powers.

Glen Weissenberger

2017

Editor, *The Protection of Magicians' Secrets*, (The World Alliance of Magicians, Inc., 2000).

Legal Counsel, emeritus, the International Brotherhood of Magicians.

Chairman, Legal Advisory Committee, The World Alliance of Magicians, Inc. (1998-2003).

Chairman, Board of Trustees, The Greater Cincinnati and Northern Kentucky Film Commission (2000-2002).

MIRACLES FOR SALE (1939)

As the silent film era (1885 to 1936) moved into the "Golden Age of Hollywood" (late '20s to '60s), the art and science of magic became the subject of increased attention by Hollywood moviemakers. As a result, the magical arts became accessible to middle-class, mass audiences for the first time. No longer was the best of magic reserved only for those who had both the geographic access and the means to afford a ticket to top-notch, live theatrical magic spectacles.

Miracles for Sale is based upon the novel, *Death from a Top Hat*, by amateur magician and noted "locked-room mystery" writer Clayton Rawson. Just as magic and its allied arts have innumerable variations, so do genres of fiction. The "locked-room mystery" is a sub-genre of detective fiction, one in which a significant crime (typically a murder) is committed where there is no perceivable means of the perpetrator's escaping—yet, he does! Harry Ruskin, Marlon Parsonnet, and James Edward Grant ably penned the screenplay based upon Rawson's novel, which set the stage for studio development of *Miracles for Sale*.

Miracles' director, Tod Browning, was widely known for his dark and bizarre films. Browning was a frequent collaborator with Lon Chaney during the silent film era, with several of his films from the 1930s and '40s becoming cult classics that continue to define the horror genre. Before *Miracles for Sale*, Browning was particularly well known for directing the classic monster film *Dracula* (1931), starring Bela Lugosi, as well as for directing the controversial and disturbing film *Freaks* (1932). Browning's filmography reveals a wide range of genres in which he worked as a director, actor, and screenwriter. Consequently, a detective locked-room mystery featuring a magician as the central character was well within his wheelhouse. *Miracles for Sale* was Browning's last film before entering self-imposed seclusion. It was also the last of six films in which Robert Young and Florence Rice starred opposite one another as romantic partners.

The movie's plot cast Young in the role of a magician (Michael Morgan) who, for a living, invents and sells stage illusions for other magicians. His genuine passion, however, is exposing performers who steal illusions from the artists who originated them. In a clever and fast-moving plot, a mysterious individual threatens Rice's character (Judy Barclay), and Young's effort to protect her leads them to solve a double murder—a seeming unsolvable one—directly thanks to Morgan's skills as a magician.

Florence Rice never became a major figure in film, even though she appeared in almost twenty studio movies between 1934 and 1943. Robert Young, a contract actor with Metro-Goldwyn-Mayer at the height of the studio system, was cast in over 100 films between 1931 and 1951, frequently appearing in six to eight movies per year. However, Young will be most remembered for his Emmy Award winning television roles in *Father Knows Best* (1954-60) and *Marcus Welby, M.D.* (1969-76).

Miracles for Sale was favorably reviewed by critics at the time of its initial release. "This whodunit has some background color that tickles the imagination [and] leaves a pleasant impression," noted *Variety*. Frank Nugent wrote in the *New York Times*, "[T]he tale has been told rather ingeniously, and jogs along briskly under Tod Browning's direction." Alfred Eaker, following the 2011 video release, called *Miracles* "an underrated charmer." Nevertheless, in what would become a point of ongoing tension and debate in the matter of moviemakers and magicians, The Pacific Coast Association of Magicians (PCAM) publicly criticized the film for exposing the secrets of several magical effects.

Miracles for Sale is packed with magic. It has a first-rate cast, with Young and Rice displaying genuine real chemistry. The story unfolds briskly, with a few intriguing magical and mysterious plot twists. This is a film worth finding and watching.

MOVIE CREDITS

Director	Tod Browning
Based upon	Clayton Rawson's novel *Death from a Top Hat* (1938)
Adapted Screenplay	Harry Ruskin Marion Parsonnet James Edward Grant
Producer	J. J. Cohn
Production Company	Metro-Goldwyn-Mayer
Featured Cast	Robert Young Florence Rice Frank Craven Henry Hull
Composer	William Axt
Cinematographer	Charles Lawton, Jr.
Editor	Fredrick Y. Smith
Distributor	Metro-Goldwyn-Mayer
U.S. Release date	August 10, 1939 (New York, New York)
Running time	71 minutes

MPAA rating	NR
B/W or Color	B/W
Where to Find?	*Miracles for Sale* is available for purchase from Amazon in DVD format as part of the Warner Bros. Archive Collection, "Robert Young: Wac X2 Feature (2 Discs)."

ETERNALLY YOURS (1939)

M OTION PICTURE AND FILM HISTORIANS agree that 1939 was a banner year in Hollywood cinema. It is not surprising that 1939's modest films, such as the detective-mystery, *Miracles for Sale*, and the screwball comedy, *Eternally Yours*, were eclipsed by the amazingly robust slate of 1939 movies that have become all-time classics.

In 1939, the Academy of Motion Picture Arts and Sciences (AMPAS) remarkably nominated a total of ten films for its 1940 Best Picture award. Moreover, record-breaking crowds drove 1939 box office receipts to historic highs, as audiences flocked to superb film adaptations of Sir Arthur Conan Doyle's *The Hound of the Baskervilles*, Emily Brontë's *Wuthering Heights*, and James Hilton's *Goodbye Mr. Chips*. In August 1939, the fantastic delights of *The Wizard of Oz* premiered at the legendary Grauman's Chinese Theater on Hollywood Boulevard, and in October 1939, Frank Capra's charming *Mr. Smith's Going to Washington* opened in Washington, D.C.

Even among such august company, one film stands as 1939's far-and-away most popular by every measure. With its over-the-top, three-day December 1939 premiere and accompanying festival in Atlanta, Georgia, *Gone with the Wind* made its debut. David O. Selznick's film—as epic as Margaret Mitchell's 1936 novel of the same name—swept the 1940 Academy Awards, with only a few exceptions: the Oscar for Best Music, Original Score went to Werner Janssen, the composer and musical director for the quirky, character-driven *Eternally Yours*.

Unfortunately, *Eternally Yours* is hampered by a convoluted plot. Otherwise, it could be appreciated as an endearing, witty romance in which David Niven plays the charming, but wildly irresponsible stage magician and fortune teller, Tony, aka "The Great Arturo." Arturo successfully wiles Anita Halstead (Loretta Young) from her engagement to the staid and conventional Don Burns (Broderick Crawford). Mutually smitten, they marry and then embark on an around-the-world tour of Arturo's magic act. Predictably, Arturo's peripatetic lifestyle and insensitivity takes its toll on Anita. While Arturo is delighting in the glow of the limelight and performing ever more Houdini-esque stunts—such as jumping out of a plane while handcuffed—he loses Anita to Don. The balance of the film is an amusing joust between the men to win Anita's heart forever.

Eternally Yours received praise for the superb acting of its two leads, who in 1939 were both emerging stars. David Niven shines in one of his first roles as a leading man. He brings his gentility to what otherwise could have been a mere caricature of Arturo. Loretta Young, in her first film after losing her contract with 20th Century Fox, "gives a warm, witty performance," according to the *Turner Classic Movies* website. Both Niven and Young would go on to win Academy Awards for subsequent roles. Here, their sentimental and comedic efforts are revealed in the witty repartee which results in electrifying chemistry between them.

Particularly noteworthy is footage in *Eternally Yours* from the 1939 New York World's Fair and magician Paul LePaul's (the film's technical advisor) cameo doing card tricks.

Eternally Yours is well worth seeing for its playful, clever magical romps, and a glimpse at early performances by actors who would go on to become genuine Hollywood stars.

MOVIE CREDITS

Director   Tay Garnett

Technical Advisor,   Paul LePaul
Magic

Original Screenplay	Gene Towne Graham Baker
Producer	Tay Garnett
Production Company	Walter Wagner Productions
Featured Cast	David Niven Loretta Young Broderick Crawford
Composer and Musical Director	Werner Janssen
Cinematographer	Merritt B. Gerstad
Editors	Otho Lovering Dorothy Spencer
Distributor	United Artists
U.S. Release date	October 7, 1939 (New York, New York)
Running time	95 minutes
MPAA rating	NR
B/W or Color	B/W
Where to Find?	*Eternally Yours* is available for purchase from Amazon in DVD format. For online viewing, the film is available to rent or to buy from Amazon Video (in SD/HD formats).

Additionally, a copyright dispute resulted in *Eternally Yours* falling into public domain; it is available for free online viewing on the Public Domain Entertainment's YouTube channel.

THE MASK OF DIIJON (1946)

*T*HE *MASK OF DIIJON* would have become a forgotten film were it not for its star, Erich von Stroheim. Von Stroheim's career began in the silent film era and reached its peak with his Oscar-nominated performance in Billy Wilder's *Sunset Boulevard* (1950). Promoted as the "man you love to hate," von Stroheim was a director, writer, and actor, with his best-known acting role in Jean Renoir's *La Grande Illusion* (1957).

Von Stroheim's Diijon is an embittered magician who abandons his career to pursue the study of hypnosis. He neglects his pretty wife and stage assistant, Victoria (Jeanne Bates). Left in financial straits, Victoria is vulnerable to the attentions of a younger man, Tony (William Wright), a piano-player at the local club. To secure Victoria's comfort, Tony convinces his boss to hire Diijon to perform his cobbled-together hypnosis act. To his complete humiliation, Diijon's performance dramatically backfires on opening night.

Diijon's failure triggers raging paranoia. He suspects Victoria of cheating on him with Tony, and he turns his magical talents to bring about Tony and Victoria's destruction. The end results are disastrous and spectacular, not just for others, but for Diijon himself.

The film is based on a previously-unpublished story by Arthur St. Claire, who, with Griffin Jay, wrote the screenplay. *Diijon*'s director, Lew Landers, had established himself firmly within the horror genre with 1935's *The Raven*, staring Boris Karloff and Bela Lugosi. Shortly before *Diijon*, he had directed *The Return of the Vampire* (1943).

Several critics consider *The Mask of Diijon* worth viewing simply for von Stroheim's over-the-top performance as the diabolical title character.

As a low-budget gothic horror film, *The Mask of Diijon* represents one of the better films of this genre.

———

MOVIE CREDITS

Director	Lew Landers
Story by	Arthur St. Claire
Screenplay	Arthur St. Claire Griffin Jay
Producers	Max Alexander Alfred Stern
Production Company	Producers Releasing Corporation (PRC)
Featured Cast	Erich von Stroheim Jeanne Bates William Wright
Composer	Karl Hajos
Cinematographer	Jack Greenhalgh
Editor	Roy V. Livingston
Distributor	Producers Releasing Corporation (PRC)
U.S. Release date	March 7, 1946
Running time	73 minutes
MPAA rating	NR

B/W or Color   B/W

Where to Find?   *The Mask of Diijon* is available for purchase
                                from Amazon in DVD format.

NIGHTMARE ALLEY (1947)

TYRONE POWER, star of *Nightmare Alley*, was quoted as saying, "I'm sick of these knights-in-shining-armor parts. I want to do something worthwhile, like plays and films that have something to say." Consequently, it is not surprising he became the driving force behind the making of *Nightmare Alley*, in which his character is the antithesis of a knight-in-shining-armor. Power bought the rights to William Lindsay Gresham's 1946 novel of the same name, and then persuaded Darryl Zanuck and 20th Century Fox to make the film.

Nightmare Alley was not met with instant success. The film's subject matter—the grit of carnival life—was apparently too sordid for post-World War II audiences. Also, moviegoers were undoubtedly deterred by the harshly negative reviews, such as the one that appeared in the *New York Times*:

> If one can take any moral value out of *Nightmare Alley*, it would seem to be that a terrible retribution is the inevitable consequence for he who would mockingly attempt to play God. Otherwise, the experience would not be very rewarding, for, despite some fine and intense acting by Mr. Power and others, this film traverses distasteful dramatic ground, and only rarely does it achieve any substance as entertainment.

Despite its initial anemic performance at the box office, *Nightmare Alley* is now regarded as an enduring classic film of the noir genre. According to the *Internet Movie Database* (IMDb) website, it is currently rated as one of the five best films of 1947, a list that noticeably fails to include the 1947 winner of the Academy Award for Best Picture, *A Gentleman's Agreement*.

Nightmare Alley's central character, Stanton Carlisle (Power), is an orphan who finds his way to a traveling carnival, an environment that well suits his charismatic personality. He initially becomes an apprentice to Zeena (Joan Blondell), who performs a mind-reading act with her alcoholic husband, Pete (Ian Keith), a man who is rarely sufficiently sober to perform his role in the act. Before his descent into alcoholic oblivion, Pete had been a successful vaudeville mentalist who had developed a priceless mentalist code with Zeena. When Stanton makes an innocent mistake that causes Pete's death, he seduces Zeena into revealing the code. But Stanton falls in love with Molly (Coleen Gray), a beautiful young misfit in the world of carnies. Her talent is the ability to have electricity pass through her body while wearing a skimpy costume—the abbreviated nature of her wardrobe necessary because the bolts of electricity could ignite the fabric. Stanton and Molly marry and leave the world of carnivals with knowledge of the code.

From this point, the entire atmosphere of *Nightmare Alley* changes to the elegant, if not glitzy, world of nightclub venues in which Stanton and Molly perform, using the code with effortless precision. During a performance, Stanton meets a psychiatrist named Ritter (Helen Walker) with whom he develops tricks designed to swindle the social elite of Chicago. True to the noir genre, this outright corruption pushes Stanton's life into an inevitable spiraling decline.

The movie is rich in its treatment of mentalism as a form of entertainment. Central to the plot is a mentalist's code that enables the performer to divine objects from audience members using intricate verbal cues known only to the performer and the assistant. The format of the act dates back at least to performances by Jean-Eugène Robert-Houdin (1805-1871) and his son. The mentalist's assistant moves through the venue and asks the performer to describe objects offered by members of the audience; the mentalist responds with surprising accuracy.

Of symbolic significance in the movie is the depiction of the "carnival geek," who is only ever seen as a shadow. Occupying the lowest social stratum of carnies, the geek is the most savage character in the carnival. He drunkenly bites the heads off chickens, something the carnival's audience finds curiously entertaining. The geek's symbolism in the film becomes clear in the final scenes, during which Stanton eagerly accepts the job of the geek upon crashing to rock-bottom destitution.

William Lindsay Gresham, author of the novel on which the film is based, has been described as a tormented man who well understood the consequences of alcohol abuse, a subject repeatedly examined in *Nightmare Alley*. He was fascinated by the underbelly of human existence, and saw carnival life as a microcosm of society at large. In his youth, Gresham was a frequent visitor of the sideshows of Coney Island and was transfixed by them, by magic, and by magicians. He wrote *Houdini: The Man Who Walked Through Walls* (1959) with the assistance of the well-known skeptic James Randi. His lost battle with alcoholism was the ultimate catalyst for his wife's leaving him for famed author C. S. Lewis—an affair dramatized in the play and film *Shadowlands* (1993)—and contributed to his death by suicide at the age of fifty-three.

Now regarded as a masterfully crafted noir classic, the film contains Power's finest performance. The appreciation of *Nightmare Alley* was long arrested by its initial critical reception. Additionally, it was unavailable for reevaluation for decades due to a copyright dispute. Now available on DVD as part of 20th Century Fox's *Fox Film Noir* series, *Nightmare Alley* enjoys a rare 100% rating on the *Rotten Tomatoes* website, and should not be missed.

——

Movie Credits

Director	Edmund Goulding
Based upon	William Lindsay Gresham's novel *Nightmare Alley* (1946)
Adapted Screenplay	Jules Furthman

Producer	George Jessell
Production Company	20th Century Fox
Featured Cast	Tyrone Power Coleen Gray Joan Blondell Helen Walker
Composer	Cyril J. Mockridge
Cinematographer	Lee Garmes
Editor	Barbara McLean
Distributor	20th Century Fox
U.S. Release date	October 9, 1947 (New York, New York)
Running time	110 minutes
MPAA rating	NR
B/W or Color	B/W
Where to Find?	*Nightmare Alley* is available for purchase from Amazon in DVD and Blu-ray formats. For online viewing, *Nightmare Alley* is available to rent or to buy from Amazon Video (in SD/HD formats).

LILI (1953)

*L*ILI HAS BEEN CALLED "a little masterpiece" and described with terms like "tender," "charming," and "enchanting." Charles Walters' direction has been called "impeccable," and the screenplay by Helen Deutsch has been lauded as "superb" and "moving." Every member of the cast received nearly unanimous praise, but virtually every reviewer credited Leslie Caron's portrayal of Lili Daurier as the foremost reason the film has an unforgettable quality that rivals that of classic fairy tales.

Bosley Crowther, noted *New York Times* critic, enthusiastically praised the entire production, but singled out Caron, "Leslie Caron's simplicity and freshness...have been captured again in the film." Obviously impressed by Ms. Caron's performance, he used such terms as "elfin," "winsome," and "the focus of warmth and appeal" to describe her. Others have described her qualities as "charming," "beautiful," and "graceful."

Lili has occasionally been called a small film, perhaps because of its inevitable comparison to the earlier *An American in Paris* (1951), in which Ms. Caron had been personally chosen by Gene Kelly to play Lise Bouvier. When selected, Ms. Caron was a professional dancer, but she had never before appeared in film. Most certainly, *An American in Paris* was a big film, with the star power of Gene Kelly, ten musical segments and several hit songs (e.g., "Embraceable You," "Nice Work If You Can Get It," "I Got Rhythm," "Our Love Is Here to Stay," and "'S Wonderful"). *An American in Paris* received six Academy Awards, including Best Picture.

The screenplay for *Lili* was adapted from "The Man Who Hated People," a short story by Paul Gallico that first appeared in the *Saturday Evening Post* in 1950. Lili, a young, naïve girl, arrives in a provincial town expecting to be employed in a shop owned by a friend of her deceased father. The shop has closed because of the owner's recent death, and Lili finds employment in another shop, where the new proprietor tries to take advantage of her. Lili is rescued by a carnival magician, Marc (Jean-Pierre Aumont), who helps her find work as a waitress. Lili is infatuated with Marc, but soon learns that he has romantic entanglements. Disheartened, she is comforted by the carnival's puppeteer, Paul Berthalet (Mel Ferrer), who speaks to her through his puppets. Soon, Lili becomes part of the puppet show, and as the story unfolds, the puppeteer expresses his heartfelt emotions through his puppets.

On the surface, *Lili* might appear to be only a film for children, but it is also an adult love story with mature themes including vanity, self-loathing, unfulfilled dreams, and love. Successful on several levels, *Lili* has been described as "a romantic fable or a sophisticated fairy tale."

For her role in *Lili*, Ms. Caron won the British Academy of Film and Television Arts (BAFTA) Award for Best Actress in a Leading Role, and received her first of two Academy Award nominations for Best Actress—her second would be for her portrayal of Jane Fosset in *The L-Shaped Room* (1962). The film proper received a total of six Academy Award nominations, and composer Bronislau Kaper won the Oscar for Best Music (Scoring of a Dramatic or Comedy Picture). Moreover, *Lili* was the first film to become the basis for a Broadway musical, *Carnival* (1961).

While the magical effects play a minor role in the composition of the story, the magician, Marc, represents an internal counterpoint for the character of the puppeteer, Paul Berthalet. The magician is bold and brazen and very much the human centerpiece of his act. The puppeteer, in contrast, is invisible and performs only through the personae of his puppets. The polarity of these characters, and Lili's attraction to each of them, enables the audience to understand the complex development of Lili Daurier as a woman.

Strangely, *Lili* was only recently released as a DVD. It is a gem that will not disappoint any viewer.

MOVIE CREDITS

Director	Charles Walters
Based upon	Paul Gallico's short story, "The Man Who Hated People" (1950)
Adapted Screenplay	Helen Deutsch
Producer	Edwin H. Knopf
Production Company	Metro-Goldwyn-Mayer
Featured Cast	Leslie Caron Mel Ferrer Jean-Pierre Aumont Zsa Zsa Gabor
Composer	Bronislau Kaper
Cinematographer	Robert H. Planck
Editor	Ferris Webster
Distributor	Metro-Goldwyn-Mayer
U.S. Release date	March 10, 1953 (New York, New York)
Running time	81 minutes
MPAA rating	NR

B/W or Color   Color

Where to Find?   *Lili* is available for purchase from Amazon in DVD format.

                      For online viewing, the film is available to rent or to buy from Amazon Video (in SD format), iTunes, YouTube, and Google Play.

HOUDINI (1953)

Houdini was unquestionably the most legendary magician of the early twentieth century. His life has been the subject of numerous books, and while there have been several portrayals of his life in film, George Pal's 1953 biopic is the best known.

Starring Tony Curtis and Janet Leigh, *Houdini* is the first film in which the married-in-real-life couple appeared together. Although Leigh was the bigger star at the time, Leigh and Curtis received equal billing. Many film historians believe *Houdini* launched Curtis' career and that his performance as the magical icon was genuinely charismatic. Many critics also cite the believable chemistry between Leigh and Curtis as one of the movie's greatest strengths.

George Pal, the producer, was renowned for his flair for fantastic adventures, and his films *The War of the Worlds* (1953) and *The Time Machine* (1960) are among his best-known projects. According to Shep Hyken on *Houdini, the Movie* website, Pal was on a promotional tour for *When Worlds Collide* (1951) when he and his wife attended a matinee performance by Dante the Magician in San Francisco, which inspired him to consider making a film about a magician. Houdini was the first performer who came to mind. Pal, whose interest in magic dated back to his childhood, pursued the rights to produce the film. After clearing away some legal obstacles, Pal approached virtually every studio in Hollywood to make the movie. Ultimately, Pal convinced Paramount to make *Houdini* based on Harold Kellock's biography, *Houdini: His life-story* (1928). Thereafter, George Marshall (*Destiny Rides Again*, 1939; *How the West Was Won*, 1962) signed on as director.

Houdini was a huge financial success, and it remains a wonderful family film for contemporary audiences. Even the critical reviews were tepidly favorable. *Variety*'s review is representative:

A typical screen biography, presenting a rather fanciful version of Houdini's life. Production does well by illusions and escapes on which Houdini won his fame, using these tricks to give substance to a lot that uses a backstage formula that follows pat lines. Under George Marshall's direction, the story spins along nicely, with occasional emphasis on drama in several escape sequences to keep interest up. Performances of two stars are likeable, although neither shows any aging in the time span that covers Houdini from twenty-one to death.

The film's box office success is undoubtedly traceable to the casting of the recently married Curtis and Leigh. According to the *Turner Classic Movies* website:

Casting newlyweds Curtis and Leigh was a publicity coup for Paramount, as the public was fascinated by the young marrieds and was eager to see them together on screen. Both were under contract to other studios, so Paramount had to negotiate loan-outs: Curtis from Universal, Leigh from MGM. As a result of the complex contracts, according to Curtis's autobiography, 'The studios got a lot of money for it, but we just got our regular salaries.'

It is now widely known that *Houdini* is a highly fictionalized account of the man originally known as Erik Weisz. The *Turner Classic Movies* website captures the essence of the story:

Houdini is an excellent example of a biography that remains true to the spirit of an historical character even as it fictionalizes most of the facts of his life, including his demise. The script by the prolific Philip Yordan pays homage to the mystique of Harry Houdini, a man who had half the world believing he possessed supernatural powers.

While audiences and contemporary magicians appear unbothered by multiple historical inaccuracies in the script, magicians at the time of the film's release in 1953 were highly critical of its frequent departures from reality. Magician, magic historian, and Houdini biographer Milbourne Christopher, in *Houdini: The Untold Story* (1976), spoke for many of his colleagues when he said:

> I won't attempt to list the anachronisms and inaccuracies in the film. Generally speaking, if any phase of Houdini's life is shown on the screen, you can be sure it didn't happen the ways it's pictured.

It has been speculated among present-day magicians that Christopher was piqued by the selection of Joseph Dunninger as the technical consultant for the movie. As a masterful showman, Dunninger was well known for exaggeration and prevarication. Dunninger claimed to have been a close friend of Houdini, an assertion that has been called into question. Moreover, according to the *Wild About Harry* website:

> Dunninger receives a lavish credit as technical advisor, but according to Tony Curtis, the true technical advisor on the film was George Boston. 'Dunninger was a blowhard,' Curtis would tell a Magic Castle audience in 2009. And speaking of the Magic Castle, that's cofounder Bill Larsen, Jr. [uncredited] performing the guillotine act at the SAM [the Society of American Magicians] convention in the film.

On the *Turner Classic Movies* website Curtis further discounts Dunninger's role:

> Curtis remembered that he trained for the role not under Dunninger, but under magician George Boston. 'I worked with him every day for about four months before the picture started on escapes and sleight of hand. I was a pretty quick study, and it stayed with me for life. I still practice it, and I've been inducted into the Magicians Society here and in Japan.'

George L. Boston was an accomplished magician and an assistant to Houdini's contemporary, Howard Thurston.

Notwithstanding various points of criticism, Shep Hyken, on *Houdini, the Movie* website, aptly describes the great significance of *Houdini*:

> Of all the movies and documentaries on the life of the great Harry Houdini over the years, none have had the acclaim and international exposure of George Pal's *Houdini*, starring Tony Curtis and Janet Leigh…Hollywood and the entertainment industry are different than they were fifty years ago. Back then, movies were major events. Stars were larger than life. That era of show business may be gone forever, but its movies live on. As for movies about magic and magicians, there may not be any others as successful, wide-reaching, and glamorous as *Houdini*. *Houdini* is, without a doubt, one of magic's greatest movies—ever!

MOVIE CREDITS

Director	George Marshall
Technical Advisor, Magic	Joseph Cunningham
Based upon	Harold Kellock's biography *Houdini: His life-story* (1928)
Adapted Screenplay	Philip Yordan
Producers	George Pal Berman Swarttz Frank Freeman, Jr.

Production Company	Paramount Pictures
Featured Cast	Tony Curtis Janet Leigh Torin Thatcher
Composer	Roy Webb
Cinematographer	Ernest Laszlo
Editor	George Tomasini
Distributor	Paramount Pictures
U.S. Release date	July 2, 1953
Running time	106 minutes
MPAA rating	Approved
B/W or Color	Color
Where to Find?	*Houdini* is available for purchase from Amazon in DVD and Blu-ray formats. For online viewing, the film is available to rent or to buy from Amazon Video (in SD/HD formats), iTunes, YouTube, Google Play, and Vudu. For free online viewing, Paramount Pictures has made the full movie available on its YouTube channel.

THE MAD MAGICIAN (1954)

DON GALLICO (VINCENT PRICE) is a master magical illusion designer and builder whose creations are sold by his employer, Ross Ormond (Donald Randolph), to master magicians such as The Great Rinaldi (John Emery). Gallico yearns to perform his creations himself, and when he finally mounts a show, Ormond and his lawyer deliver a cease-and-desist order against Gallico's performance of the "Buzz Saw" illusion. Enraged by the use of legal technicalities to shut down his act, Gallico embarks on a campaign to employ his magical apparatuses to seek revenge against those who have wronged him. The resulting maniacal behavior involves beheadings, clever masks and disguises, strangulations, a cremation, and other miscellaneous mayhem.

The Mad Magician has been seen as Columbia Pictures' effort to capitalize on the success of *House of Wax* (1952). Both movies star Vincent Price, both were shot in 3-D, and both had the same producer (Bryan Foy), cinematographer (Bert Glennon), and writer (Crane Wilbur). Regrettably, most critics found *The Mad Magician* a weak effort to replicate the successful qualities of *House of Wax*.

Vincent Price had a lasting association with the horror genre, but he began his career as a character actor, appearing in such films as *Brigham Young* (1940) and *Laura* (1944). By the 1950s, Price, however, was well established as a horror film actor, a genre in which he would work through the 1970s. In his later career, Price capitalized on his image with campy performances, providing voiceover work, such as his turn as "Vincent Van Ghoul" in the 1985-86 television series *The 13 Ghosts of Scooby-Doo*. It would be fair to state that a film like *The Mad Magician* would never have been made were it not for the strong identity of Vincent Price with horror films such as *House of Wax*.

While *The Mad Magician* was probably produced with no pretense of being anything other than a B-movie, a number of the film's attributes warrant its viewing by contemporary audiences. Price delivers a controlled, if not understated, performance that is quite believable. The supporting cast provides entertaining, but not necessarily memorable, performances. The plot is certainly clever enough to hold the movie together to its conclusion. And some entertaining magic is performed, most notably a sequence involving intricate, pneumatically-produced liquid effects. Finally, it was an early 3-D film, and it is worth watching for this special effect alone.

Movie Credits

Director	John Brahm
Original Screenplay	Crane Wilbur
Producer	Bryan Foy
Production Company	Columbia Pictures
Featured Cast	Vincent Price Mary Murphy Eva Gabor
Composers	Arthur Lange Emil Newman
Cinematographer	Bert Glennon
Editor	Grant Whytock
Distributor	Columbia Pictures

U.S. Release date	May 19, 1954 (New York, New York)
Running time	72 minutes
MPAA rating	Unrated
B/W or Color	B/W
Where to Find?	*The Mad Magician* is available for purchase from Amazon in DVD and 3D Blu-ray formats, and in a "Classic Horror 4 Movie Pack" DVD set.
	For free online viewing, see screenwriter Crane Wilbur's archives, https://archive.org/details/TheMad Magician/

THE GEISHA BOY (1958)

*T*HE *GEISHA BOY* is the fourth of eight collaborations between comedic actor Jerry Lewis and director Frank Tashlin. As one reviewer stated, "Lewis still remains a love-it-or-loathe-it proposition for modern-era filmgoers—but there is no denying his legacy and impact on the contemporary comedy scene." *The Geisha Boy* represents a Lewis classic and an example of some of his finest solo work apart from Dean Martin.

Lewis plays Gilbert Wooley, variously described by reviewers as "a down-on-his-luck magician," "an unsuccessful magician," "a second-rate magician," "a fifth-rate magician," and "a third-rate USO magician." With no prospects of work, his agent books him on a USO tour in Japan. Despite his lack of skill as a magician, it turns out that Wooley is the only person who can make an orphaned Japanese boy laugh. The boy's aristocratic grandfather, played by Sessue Hayakawa, salvages Wooley's career. An international incident nearly develops when the young boy tries to follow Wooley back to the United States, and Wooley is accused of kidnapping. The film is loaded with sight gags and the usual Lewis shtick, but it also contains scenes that allow Lewis to demonstrate that he can effectively convey serious, warmhearted emotion.

The film opened in 1959 with favorable reviews and handsome box office receipts. It remains a sentimental favorite for many, particularly those seeking genuine family fare. Several aspects of *The Geisha Boy* make it particularly memorable. For instance, in a ballpark scene featuring various members of the 1958 Los Angeles Dodgers, including Gil Hodges, Wooley cannot understand why the Japanese crowd does not root for his favorite players. It is also Suzanne Pleshette's first film role, which launched her long, successful career. Nobu McCarthy, the orphan boy's aunt, is beautiful and restrained as she competes with Pleshette for Wooley's affections.

One of the most delightful features of the film, particularly for children, is the character of Harry Hare, who is introduced in the opening credits. Frank Tashlin, the director and a former *Looney Tunes* animator, created Harry Hare with anthropomorphic qualities. Harry rides on top of a taxicab. He floats on a raft and gets a sunburn. He tries to cure a headache with a bag of ice. He slides down a massive banister. He leans one-armed and cross-legged against a box in Bugs Bunny's signature pose.

The Geisha Boy was a big hit, and it further validated Lewis' status as a solo star after his well-known duo career with Dean Martin. It also firmly established Frank Tashlin as a premier comedic director. He masterfully gives the film a cartoonish flair, with rapid-fire iconographic gags well-placed between the more serious dialogue. Visually, Tashlin uses bold primary colors that generate a synergy with the film's action, and he often creates beautiful panoramic landscapes as transitions.

The Geisha Boy most definitely deserves its reputation as one of the great family films with ageless humor and heart.

MOVIE CREDITS

Director	Frank Tashlin
Story by	Rudy Makoul
Screenplay	Frank Tashlin
Producer	Jerry Lewis
Production Company	York Pictures Corporation

Featured Cast	Jerry Lewis Marie McDonald Suzanne Pleshette Nobu McCarthy
Composer	Walter Scharf
Cinematographer	Haskell B. Boggs
Editor	Alma Macrorie
Distributor	Paramount Pictures
U.S. Release date	December 19, 1958 (New York, New York)
Running time	98 minutes
MPAA rating	Approved
B/W or Color	Color
Where to Find?	*The Geisha Boy* is available for purchase from Amazon in DVD and Blue-ray formats, and in a "4 Film Favorites: Jerry Lewis" DVD set.
	For online viewing, the film is available to rent or to buy from Amazon Video (in SD/HD formats), Google Play, YouTube, iTunes, and Vudu.

THE MAGICIAN (ANSIKTET) (1958)

INGMAR BERGMAN, writer and director of *The Magician*, is recognized as one of the most influential auteurs of the twentieth century. Praised by virtually every highly-regarded film director, Bergman is known for his *Wild Strawberries* (1957), *The Seventh Seal* (1957), *Persona* (1966), and *Fanny and Alexander* (1982). Bergman wrote most of his own screenplays, which usually involved dark themes such as death, insanity, and illness. Three of his films won the Academy Award for Best Foreign Language Film, and he was frequently honored at the Cannes Film Festival and by BAFTA. Bergman is indisputably one of the most accomplished directors since the advent of the film industry.

The Magician (released in Sweden as *Ansiktet*, literally translated as "The Face") was made at the peak of Bergman's career. A year previous, he had completed *The Seventh Seal* and *Wild Strawberries*. A year later, Bergman would make *Virgin Spring*. While *The Magician* received high critical acclaim, it is one of Bergman's largely forgotten, overlooked films. It is not at all clear why this film is considered an outlier compared to others Bergman made during this period. Scott Tobias, on the *AV Club* website, offers the explanation that less attention was paid to *The Magician* "…because it lacks the buoyancy of his comedies and the severity of his dramas." While *The Magician* was called one of Bergman's "most challenging and uncomfortable films" in the *Gurdjieff Journal*, Dennis Grunes provides the polar opposite evaluation, "Ingmar Bergman has a reputation for making stubborn and difficult films. However, his [*The*] *Magician*…is widely regarded as one of his most accessible works."

The Magician received the Best Film prize at the British Academy Awards, the Best Foreign Film prize at the New York Film Critics Awards, and two prizes at the Venice Film Festival. Highly praised and favorably received at the time of its release, it is hard to pinpoint why it is now viewed as "lesser Bergman."

Set in the mid-1800s, *The Magician* follows a traveling illusionist and his troupe, called "Vogler's Magnetic Health Theater." Upon approaching a town, the troupe is stopped at a crossing and ordered to perform before a jury of leading townspeople. The people of the town seek to investigate reports of a variety of supernatural disturbances at Vogler's (Max von Sydow) prior performances. Among the informal jury are scientifically minded nonbelievers who try to expose the troupe as charlatans. But before the nonbelievers allow the troupe to perform publicly, they hold an informal inquest. The dichotomy of scientific explanation and supernatural manifestation frames the film's primary themes. Bergman would not, however, permit such an obvious tension to operate as the film's sole artistic examination. Much more is served up for consideration.

Most reviewers conclude that Vogler is an autobiographical figure used by Bergman to examine the illusion of film and the role of the director as he deceives his audience. Vogler is portrayed as a man tortured by anxiety, self-doubt, and depression, particularly in the presence of those who doubt him. Most reviewers also feel that virtually every character in the film symbolically represents a theoretical perspective on the role of art in understanding humanity. While the dominant characters are exaggeratedly drawn, the plot's meaning is much more subtle and obscure. Likely, the film was meant to be more of an exploration than a movie with clear messages.

The film contains several enigmatic elements (such as whether or not the ending is in fact a trick concocted by Vogler), but contrary to some interpretations, there appears to be nothing supernatural about Vogler's illusions. When a film is viewed, the audience does not understand the tricks used by the director and cinematographer to produce what is actually seen; likewise, the observer of a successful magic trick or illusion does not understand the performer's methods. Through the plot device of an elaborate melodramatic prank played on the town's medical officer, Bergman demonstrates that a person can be struck with terror by seemingly supernatural events, even when he fiercely believes that everything is subject to scientific explanation.

While it may not be the equivalent of some of Bergman's masterpieces such as *The Seventh Seal*, *The Magician* is nevertheless a great and important film. Like all Bergman, it is challenging to understand, but worth the effort.

——

MOVIE CREDITS

Director	Ingmar Bergman
Original Screenplay	Ingmar Bergman
Producer	Allan Ekelund
Production Company (Sweden)	Svensk Filmindustri
Featured Cast	Ingrid Thulin Max von Sydow Naima Wifstrand Gunnar Björnstrand
Composer	Erik Nordgren
Cinematographer	Gunnar Fischer
Editor	Oscar Rosander
U.S. Distributor	Janus Films

U.S. Release date   August 27, 1959

Running time   107 minutes

MPAA rating   Approved

B/W or Color   B/W

Where to Find?   *The Magician* is available for purchase from Amazon in multi-region DVD formats and languages, and in a Criterion Collection set.

For online viewing, the film is available to rent or to buy at Amazon Video (in HD format), iTunes, Google Play, YouTube, and Vudu.

For free online viewing, the Criterion Collection has made the full film available on its YouTube channel.

GET TO KNOW
YOUR RABBIT (1972)

GET TO KNOW YOUR RABBIT was directed by Brian De Palma, who had previously directed the well-received comedy *Greetings* (1968). Later, De Palma would become known as a director of more serious films such as *Carrie* (1976), *Scarface* (1983), *The Untouchables* (1987), and *Carlito's Way* (1993). Of all De Palma's movies, *Get to Know Your Rabbit* was considered by many as his "quirkiest" and his "most forgettable."

The storyline is in the vein of counterculture satire. Don Beeman (Tom Smothers), burned out by the pressures of his corporate job, precipitously quits and joins a school run by Mr. Delasandro (Orson Welles) that teaches its students the art of becoming tap-dancing magicians. Beeman's former boss, Mr. Turnbull (John Astin) earnestly tries to cajole Beeman into returning to his mundane job and follows Beeman as he performs at seedy clubs and strip joints. Turnbull's pursuit of Beeman becomes so obsessive that he loses his own corporate position, and he joins Beeman as his manager and ally. The two ultimately create a new school for tap-dancing magicians, a venture that develops into a huge corporate empire. Needless to say, Beeman finds himself back where he started, faced with the need to escape once again.

Get to Know Your Rabbit can only be appreciated—and perhaps even only understood—in the context of the cinematic time period of its creation. During the early 1970s, Hollywood took chances on risky projects. It has been described as a time when films could be "really weird" and "conceptually ambitious." Substantial segments of society were questioning the white-collar corporate establishment, and *Get to Know Your Rabbit* was certainly one of the more good-natured assaults— compare *A Thousand Clowns* (1965). Simultaneously, film comedy at that time was substantially derived from the traditional British absurdist sense of humor typified by *Monty Python's Flying Circus*. While perhaps *Get to Know Your Rabbit* will not stand the test of time as a great movie, it was given a quite favorable review by Vincent Canby in the *New York Times*.

There are many reasons to commend *Get to Know Your Rabbit* to modern audiences. Orson Welles' performance as Mr. Delasandro, the grand master of the seedy tap-dancing magicians' academy, is virtuosic. (While perhaps not known to general film viewers, Welles was a skilled magician with a passion for the art.) Actors John Astin and Allen Garfield are also superb. There are cul-de-sacs of incredibly clever humor, such as the morose brassiere manufacturer (Garfield) who wistfully searches for a woman who appreciates "a good medium-priced bra." Katharine Ross, identified only by the phrase "Terrific-Looking Girl," does look quite terrific while recounting a story of her crush on a newspaper boy that involved prostituting herself to afford a newspaper subscription. Nonsensical plot twists, non-sequiturs, and bizarre digressions abound, which—if properly appreciated—make the film genuinely funny.

Differences with Warner Bros. prevented De Palma from finishing the film. The studio balked at De Palma's ending, which involved Beeman hacking a rabbit in two on a live broadcast of Johnny Carson's *The Tonight Show*. Like Welles, Carson's early career involved stints as a magician, and, like Welles, he probably would have appeared in the film. The studio finished the film without De Palma. *Get to Know Your Rabbit* was never widely promoted, and if not for De Palma's subsequent success, would have been likely forgotten.

MOVIE CREDITS

Director	Brian De Palma
Original Screenplay	Jordan Crittenden
Producers	Steven Bernhardt
	Paul Gaer
Production Companies	Warner Bros. Pictures
	Acrobatic Motion Works West
Featured Cast	Tom Smothers
	John Astin
	Allen Garfield
	Katharine Ross
	Orson Welles
Composers	Jack Elliott
	Allyn Ferguson
Cinematographer	John A. Alonzo
Editors	Peter Colbert
	Frank J. Urioste
Distributor	Warner Bros. Pictures
U.S. Release date	June 30, 1972
Running time	91 minutes

MPAA rating   R

B/W or Color   Color

Where to Find?   *Get to Know Your Rabbit* is available for purchase
                        from Amazon in DVD format.

                        For online viewing, the film is available to rent
                        or to buy from Amazon Video (in SD format),
                        iTunes, YouTube, and Google Play.

THE ESCAPE ARTIST (1982)

W HILE *THE ESCAPE ARTIST* failed to find an audience at the time of its release, it has nevertheless developed a cult following over time. A charming film, its popularity is undoubtedly attributable to the entire cast's captivating performances. The chemistry between the two primary characters, Stu Quiñones (Raúl Juliá) and Danny Masters (Griffin O'Neal), is nicely orchestrated by cinematographer-turned-director Caleb Deschanel (the father of actress Zooey Deschanel). Quiñones and Masters' relationship, characterized by more than one reviewer as an "odd-couple" dynamic, has also been described as "immensely entertaining." Other characters in the film are brilliantly cast as well. Desi Arnaz, in his last film role, ably plays a despicable villain, a corrupt mayor begging to be duped. Teri Garr, while spot-on in her portrayal of Quiñones' sleazy girlfriend, does seem underutilized. Other established actors—Joan Hackett, Gabriel Dell, and Jackie Coogan—all turn in superb performances.

With laudable acting and directing, it is curious that the film was not an instant hit. Some reviewers have pointed to the plot's slender central premise as the reason for *The Escape Artist's* lack of an immediate and widespread audience reception.

Danny Masters (O'Neal) is the teenage son of a deceased famous magician. Masters picks the pocket of the son (Raúl Juliá) of a town's corrupt mayor (Desi Arnaz). Masters, an able magician in his own right, finds himself involved in a tense dynamic between the mayor and his ne'er-do-well son. While following the journey of the lost wallet—it is hidden in various places—Masters uncovers new information about his father's death and sets out to avenge his legacy.

While surrounded by established actors displaying extraordinary talents, Griffin O'Neal deserves much of the credit for the film's success. Called an actor with "natural screen presence" by Vincent Canby of the *New York Times*, he creates a believable central character in a story that requires a stretch of the viewers' imaginations. Moreover, he trained extensively for his first movie role and performed the requisite magic escapes and illusions himself. The son of actors Ryan O'Neal and Joanna Moore, Griffin O'Neal showed great promise as a Hollywood star. He appeared in a few film roles after *The Escape Artist*, but dropped out of sight in 1991. His life was plagued by tragic accidents, particularly a 1986 boating accident that took the life of Francis Ford Coppola's son, Gian-Carlo Coppola.

Followers of magic and magicians may discover some interesting aspects of the film that have eluded general film reviewers. Many of the escape scenes are staged as a tribute to similar scenes in the 1953 film *Houdini*, starring Tony Curtis and Janet Leigh. Also, Danny's father, who appears in very short sequences, is played by Harry Anderson, who later developed substantial fame as a magician and television personality.

Overall, *The Escape Artist* is a delightful film that deserves more than the B-movie status it acquired upon its initial theatrical release.

———

MOVIE CREDITS

Director	Caleb Deschanel
Based upon	David Wagoner's novel *The Escape Artist* (1965)
Adapted Screenplay	Melissa Mathison Stephen Zito
Producers	Doug Claybourne Buck Houghton
Production Company	Zoetrope Studios

Featured Cast	Raúl Juliá
	Griffin O'Neal
	Desi Arnaz
	Teri Garr
	Joan Hackett
	Harry Anderson
Composer	Georges Delerue
Cinematographer	Stephen H. Burum
Editor	Arthur Schmidt
Distributor	Orion Pictures Corporation
U.S. Release date	May 28, 1982
Running time	94 minutes
MPAA rating	PG
B/W or Color	Color
Where to Find?	*The Escape Artist* is available for purchase from Amazon in DVD format.
	For online viewing, the film is available to rent or to buy from Amazon Video (in SD/HD formats), Google Play, YouTube, and Vudu.

PENN & TELLER GET KILLED (1989)

P LAYING THEMSELVES, PENN AND TELLER make an appearance on a local New York television show, presenting themselves as the "bad boys of magic." At the conclusion of the segment, Penn remarks that he wishes someone were threatening to kill him, so that he "wouldn't sweat the small stuff." Most of the film's action involves Penn and Teller playing practical jokes on one another until the tragic ending suggested by the film's title.

Despite very clever material scattered throughout the film, *Penn & Teller Get Killed* generally failed to receive favorable reviews. It has been called a "low-concept failure." As Ralph Novak put it, "To look on the bright side, this is a buddy film with no car chases, where one buddy had no bad lines, and where the idea of a sequel seems out of the question."

Yes, the film's title should be taken literally.

Perhaps because Penn and Teller are an acquired taste, current retrospective reviewers are kinder than those who penned reviews at the time of its debut. John Kilduff, on the *Rewind* website, calls *Penn & Teller Get Killed* "[O]ne of the best movies of the '80s....This movie is a must-see." Contemporary audiences tend to know what to expect from Penn and Teller, making the film's humor more comprehensible. The movie may yet attain a cult status, with many viewers watching the film several times. According to one reviewer, "The gags grow amusingly complex as the film goes on....[t]hey are quite amusing."

One aspect of the film has been called "inexplicable:" *Penn & Teller Get Killed* was directed by Arthur Penn, famously known for his direction of *The Miracle Worker* (1962), *Bonnie and Clyde* (1967), and *Little Big Man* (1970). In fact, *Penn & Teller Get Killed* was the last film he directed. While it has been rationalized as Arthur Penn's attempt to direct a film about the absurdity of authority, Arthur Penn himself stated, "I had a funny, cartoonish film in mind, and I didn't do it. I should have done it way outside of unions and all that stuff. It should have been much wilder."

Penn & Teller Get Killed is certainly a much better film than it was initially thought to be. It is also a film that provides important insight into the incredibly fascinating minds of Penn and Teller, who together have marked unique territory in the world of magic.

———

Movie Credits

Director	Arthur Penn
Original Screenplay	Penn Jillette Teller
Producer	Arthur Penn
Production Company	Lorimar Film Entertainment
Featured Cast	Penn Jillette Teller
Composer	Paul Chihara
Cinematographer	Jan Weincke
Editor	Jeffrey Wolf
Distributor	Warner Bros. Pictures
Film Festival Release date	September 14, 1989 (Toronto Film Festival)

U.S. Release date	September 22, 1989
Running time	89 minutes
MPAA rating	R
B/W or Color	Color
Where to Find?	*Penn & Teller Get Killed* is available for purchase from Amazon as a single DVD, or in various Penn & Teller DVD sets.
	For online viewing, the movie is available to rent or to buy from Amazon Video (in SD format), iTunes, You Tube, and Vudu.

MAGICIANS (2000)

M ax (Til Schweiger) aspires to be a headliner magician in Las Vegas. He teams up with a pickpocket and con artist (Fabrizio Bentivoglio), an over-the-hill professional (Alan Arkin), and an attractive waitress (Claire Forlani). Together, they embark on a road trip with many stops along the way, each of which involves a small, delightful adventure.

Regrettably, *Magicians* is a largely forgotten film. Critical reviews are impossible to find, and *Rotten Tomatoes* contains no evaluation. Customer reviews of the film are quite favorable, however, and while Arkin receives the majority of kudos, each cast member receives high praise. The plot is thin, but very warm-hearted and funny.

The film was produced in Europe, and while its original intended audience is not entirely clear, the film appears to have had American viewers, because it was picked up by Blockbuster. The fact that *Magicians* never had a theatrical release in the United States would account for its obscurity.

Magicians was directed by James Merendino, probably best known for *SLC Punk* (1998), which has a cult following. His *Magicians* is a remarkably enjoyable film, and its obscurity should not be a deterrent from seeing it.

MOVIE CREDITS

Director	James Merendino
Original Screenplay	James Merendino
Producers	Sam Maydew Peter Ward
Production Company	Sleight of Hand Productions
Featured Cast	Til Schweiger Claire Forlani Fabrizio Bentivoglio Alan Arkin
Composer	Elmo Weber
Cinematographer	Thomas L. Callaway
Editor	Ester P. Russel
Distributor	Two Left Shoes Films
U.S. Release date	December 31, 2000
Running Time	108 minutes
MPAA rating	NR
B/W or Color	Color
Where to Find?	*Magicians* is available for purchase from Amazon in DVD format (U.K. edition).

THE CURSE OF
THE JADE SCORPION (2001)

W OODY ALLEN, writer and director of *The Curse of the Jade Scorpion*, said of *Curse*, "I feel that maybe—and there are many candidates for this—but it may be the worst film I've made. I have great regrets and embarrassment."

Most critics agree with him.

The plot features Allen as an insurance investigator and Helen Hunt as an efficiency expert. They despise one another. Both are hypnotized by a nightclub magician using a jade scorpion amulet. Under a hypnotic trance, Allen's character is instructed to steal valuable jewelry. Then, as the investigator, he tries to solve the crimes, not knowing that he himself is the perpetrator. The film's plot, characters, and 1940s setting are intended to recreate a screwball comedy from that era. The cast is superb, but Allen himself, in the role of the romantic lead, is the weak link, something he has acknowledged. He pursued Tom Hanks and Robert De Niro for the part, but after they turned him down, he cast himself. Quite possibly, given his self-imposed quota of releasing one film each year, time simply ran out before he could find another actor for the role.

The film's negative reviews were not universal, and while most critics found the chemistry between Hunt and Allen lacking, others praised it. Critics found the performances of Hunt and Charlize Theron praiseworthy. Others, while conceding that *Curse* was not among Allen's best films, found it entertaining nevertheless.

As a teenager, Allen was a skilled magician, and consequently several of his films have plots involving magic and its allied arts. The centerpiece of *Curse's* plot—hypnotizing and turning innocent characters into thieves—is a clever setup for the film's farcically funny moments. Allen had used the device of a magician to create a comical premise before in *New York Stories* (1989), and would use it again in *Scoop* (2006). Even more recently, Allen examined magic from a philosophic perspective in *Magic in the Moonlight* (2014).

Curse may not be a great film, but like all of Allen's movies, it has many qualities worth appreciating. Beyond those mentioned previously, Allen masterfully spins together the cinematography by Zhao Fei, production design by Santo Loquasto, art direction by Tom Warren, set direction by Jessica Lanier, and costume design by Suzanne McCabe into a rich visual experience. Allen's body of work, of which *Curse* is a component, is definitely worthy of admiration. As stated by *UPI* critic Steve Sailer:

> Indeed, the real Woody Allen has much to be maniacal about. He was a fine athlete in his youth, the captain of his high school basketball team, a first-rate amateur magician, a consort to beautiful actresses, a movie star beloved by millions (although probably not hundreds of millions) of fans, a director and writer universally admired by his peers, and an efficient businessman who can make good movies for what *Pearl Harbor* spent on catering.

Movie Credits

Director	Woody Allen
Original Screenplay	Woody Allen
Producer	Letty Aronson
Production Companies	DreamWorks Gravier Productions

Featured Cast	Woody Allen
	Helen Hunt
	Dan Akyroyd
	Brian Markinson
	Wallace Shawn
	David Ogden Stiers
	Charlize Theron
	Elizabeth Berkley
Music Department	Jill Meyers
Cinematographer	Zhao Fei
Editor	Alisa Lepselter
Distributor	DreamWorks Distribution
Film Festival Release date	August 5, 2001 (Hollywood Film Festival)
U.S. Release date	August 24, 2001
Running time	103 minutes
MPAA rating	PG-13
B/W or Color	Color
Where to Find?	*The Curse of the Jade Scorpion* is available for purchase from Amazon in DVD and Blu-ray formats.
	For online viewing, the film is available to rent or to buy from Amazon Video (in HD format), iTunes, YouTube, Vudu, and Google Play.

FUNNY VALENTINE (2005)

*F*UNNY *VALENTINE* is an obscure independent film starring Anthony Michael Hall, who appeared as a teen star in *National Lampoon's Vacation* (1983), *Sixteen Candles* (1984), *The Breakfast Club* (1985), and *Weird Science* (1985), all of which were directed by John Hughes.

The press kit for *Funny Valentine* relays the plot:

Josh [Hall] is a street performer who has trouble meeting women. His friends Sean and Tim have no trouble at all, and they set out to help Josh in ways that aren't all that helpful. Along the way, Josh discovers that all he needs is a little confidence. He builds up the courage to ask out the waitress at their local hangout and shows his friends that love is more than a good pickup line. Josh's street performances involve dressing like Charlie Chaplin and performing magic tricks.

The few available reviews of the film are generally quite negative, with most criticism directed toward the supporting cast members. Hall and his love interest, played by Marlo Marron, at times appear to have a sweet chemistry, but little else in the film is worthy of positive comment. Even with veteran editor Robert M. Reitano (*My Blue Heaven*, 1990; *Sleepless in Seattle*, 1993), the movie flows badly, with short, choppy scenes.

As one critic said, "Hall's tidy performance is doomed to be forever lost in the swampy backwaters of cinematic mediocrity."

Movie Credits

Director	Jeff Oppenheim
Original Screenplay	Jeff Oppenheim
Producers	Lloyd Chrein Leo Leichter
Production Company	Big Fresh Pictures
Featured Cast	Anthony Michael Hall Marlo Marron Ivan Martin Lord Jamar
Composer	Greg Arnold
Cinematographer	Stephen Treadway
Editor	Robert M. Reitano
Distributor	Xenon Pictures
Film Festival Release date	February 4, 2005 (Sarasota Film Festival)
U.S. Release date	January 4, 2006
Running time	90 minutes
MPAA rating	R

B/W or Color

Color

Where to Find?

Funny Valentine is available for purchase from Amazon in DVD format.

For online viewing, the movie is available to rent or to buy from Amazon Video (in SD format).

THE ILLUSIONIST (2006)

TOGETHER WITH *SCOOP* AND *THE PRESTIGE*, *The Illusionist* was one of three major American films released in 2006 with magicians as central characters. While *Scoop* and *The Prestige* are definitely worth watching, only *The Illusionist* meets the criteria for inclusion in this book.

Loosely based on the short story by Pulitzer Prize-winning novelist Steven Millhauser, "Eisenheim the Illusionist," the film's plot features Edward Norton as Eisenheim, who falls in love with a woman above his social standing, played by Jessica Biel. Eisenheim uses his magical skill to secure the noblewoman's love, despite her engagement to the crown prince Leopold (Rufus Sewell), and despite Chief Inspector Walter Uhl's (Paul Giamatti) surveillance of Eisenheim.

Set in turn-of-the-century Vienna, the film was shot mostly in the Czech Republic. Locations used included Český Krumlov as Eisenheim's childhood village, the historical fortress Konopiste as the crown prince's castle, and Prague Castle as Leopold's Vienna palace. The relatively inexperienced director Neil Burger and cinematographer Dick Pope created a film that has been called "utterly gorgeous" and "exquisitely crafted." The film received an Academy Award nomination for Best Cinematography, but lost to *Pan's Labyrinth* (2006).

The cast's performances received near-unanimous praise from critics. The only element of the film that has been criticized by some reviewers is the plot—more precisely, the ending, which some found predictable. This view, however, is in the minority. Most critics agreed with Lou Lumenick of the *New York Post*, "...[I]t is a true work of art....It's positively magical, the reason we loved movies in the first place," and with Bill Gallo in the *Village Voice*, "Beautifully acted and handsomely mounted, this gorgeous period piece is an intelligent and intriguing exploration of the 'darker arts.'"

Stephen Holden's review in the *New York Times* had praise for the entire film and insightfully points out what makes *The Illusionist* so extraordinary:

> Magic usually doesn't translate well onto the screen, since the movies themselves are larger-than-life illusions projected through thin air, especially in the age of computer-generated special effects, when every image is susceptible to endless manipulation. But the surreal, spiritualist feats Eisenheim executes, undiluted by obvious cinematographic embellishment, still produce a 'wow' effect on the screen, because they have an aesthetic elegance that transcends trickery. Even if they're fake, they look like works of art.

Unlike the plots of 2006's other two films about stage magicians, the magic performed in *The Illusionist* was not accomplished by supernatural powers. The plot specifically depends on the premise that the illusions performed are the result of Eisenheim's mortal genius, not his occult powers. However, whether the feats of magic depicted could actually have been performed with the existing technology of the late 1800s and the early 1900s is a more nuanced question that engendered an extended debate on the message boards of the *Internet Movie Database* (IMDb). The prevailing view among the posts, especially from individuals with some experience with magic, is that the illusions were historically accurate. As stated by Bill Gallo in the *Village Voice*:

> Unaided by computer effects, the tricks we see here are all 'real'— or as real as magic gets—thanks to the oversight of technical consultant Ricky Jay, who is one of the world's most accomplished sleight of hand performers and a magic historian of such perfectionist bent that these illusions are all period-accurate to the last detail.

Mr. Jay played an important role in the film's production, as did other magic consultants including James Freedman, Michael Weber, and Scott Penrose. Director Neil Burger wrote in *Magic Week*:

> Starting in pre-production, James [Freedman] became a major collaborator: brainstorming, designing, and refining everything from small sleight of hand tricks to major narrative set pieces. He worked with Edward Norton, preparing him for his stage performances, and acted as a hand double in various scenes.

Penrose, who collaborated with Freedman, is known for his work on other films and projects such as *Is Anybody There?* (2008) and *Death Defying Acts* (2008). Michael Weber is a frequent collaborator with Ricky Jay, his business partner. Together, Weber and Jay formed Deceptive Practices in the early 1990s, providing "arcane knowledge on a need-to-know basis" to film, television, and theatrical productions.

The Illusionist was a critical and financial success. It should not be missed.

MOVIE CREDITS

Director	Neil Burger
Magic Consultants	James Freedman Scott Penrose Ricky Jay Michael Weber
Based upon	Steven Millhauser's short story "Eisenheim the Illusionist"
Adapted Screenplay	Neil Burger

Producers	Brian Koppelman
	David Levien
	Michael London
	Cathy Schulman
	Bob Yari
Production Companies	Bullseye Entertainment
	Bob Yari Productions
Featured Cast	Edward Norton
	Paul Giamatti
	Jessica Biel
	Rufus Sewell
Composer	Philip Glass
Cinematographer	Dick Pope
Editor	Naomi Geraghty
Distributor	Freestyle Releasing
Film Festival Release date	January 22, 2006 (Sundance Film Festival)
U.S. Release date	September 1, 2006
Running time	110 minutes
MPAA rating	PG-13
B/W or Color	Color

Where to Find?

The Illusionist is available for purchase from Amazon in DVD and Blu-ray formats.

Online viewing of *The Illusionist* is available with a subscription to Showtime through Amazon Video.

SMOKIN' ACES (2006)

SMOKIN' ACES is a unique drama starring Jeremy Piven as the Las Vegas strip magician Buddy "Aces" Israel. Israel's profession has nothing to do with the plot, and magic has no role of any consequence in the film.

The film received universally negative reviews. *Rotten Tomatoes*, for example, called it "a violent mess of a movie." Richard Schickel wrote in *Time*, "We just sit there numbly, awaiting the next sensation and trying, without notable success, to comprehend the preposterous backstory."

Despite a veteran cast and a big budget, *Smokin' Aces* is not worth watching, especially if you are looking for magic in any form.

———

MOVIE CREDITS

Director	Joe Carnahan
Original Screenplay	Joe Carnahan
Producers	Tim Bevan
	Eric Fellner
	Noel Donnellon (title sequence)
	David Z. Obadiah (title sequence)
Production Company	Universal Pictures

Featured Cast	Jeremy Piven
	Ryan Reynolds
	Ray Liotta
	Joseph Ruskin
	Alicia Keys
Composer	Clint Mansell
Cinematographer	Mauro Fiore
Editor	Robert Frazen
Distributor	Universal Pictures
U.S. Release date	December 9, 2006
Running time	109 minutes
MPAA rating	R
B/W or Color	Color

Where to Find?

Smokin' Aces is available for purchase from Amazon in DVD and Blu-ray formats.

For online viewing, the movie is available to rent or to buy from Amazon Video (in SD/HD formats), Google Play, YouTube, iTunes, and Vudu.

For free online viewing, *Smokin' Aces* can be accessed by download at https://abc-movie.com/action/smokin-aces

DEATH DEFYING ACTS (2007)

H ARRY HOUDINI, the legendary escapologist and illusionist, is on
tour in Europe in the 1920s. He arrives in Edinburgh, preceded
by his highly-publicized pledge to pay $10,000 to any self-declared
psychic who can reveal his late mother's dying words. Eager to claim
the prize are Mary McGarvie and her daughter, Benji, two Dickensian
flimflam artists of the highest order. They ingratiate themselves into
Houdini's life in Edinburgh. During his first encounter with McGarvie,
Houdini finds her intriguing in part because of her resemblance to his
mother. McGarvie's plot to deceitfully garner the $10,000 prize becomes
subordinated to her growing infatuation with Houdini. Their unlikely
romance then dominates the film, as Houdini and McGarvie become
progressively more drawn to one another. The story endeavors to explore
the process of falling in love for two characters who live by deceit, and
whose excessively guarded personalities are reflected in their choice of
vocations.

While *Death Defying Acts* might be misperceived as docudrama, it is
clearly a work of fiction with minimal connection to actual facts. Houdini
was, of course, a larger-than-life historical figure. He has been called the
world's first superstar. Houdini did in fact perform in Edinburgh during
his European tour in the 1920s and was known to ardently endeavor
to debunk fraudulent psychics. Otherwise, with the exception of a few
inconsequential facts, the story is a complete fabrication. The distortion
of Houdini's persona in the film has actually offended many of Houdini's
admirers. One such reviewer said, "[T]he script was an affront to the
true Houdini."

Death Defying Acts' capitalization on Houdini as a historical figure
might be forgivable if the film embodied a believable romance, an

insightful psychological exploration, or an intriguing and suspenseful story. Unfortunately, it contains none of these things.

While a few critics noted the film's strengths, *Death Defying Acts* has been judged to be a mediocre film overall. Among its primary defects is that Guy Pearce (Houdini) and Catherine Zeta-Jones (McGarvie) never develop a credible chemistry. The connection between McGarvie and Houdini has been described as "bland" and "dull." Without a convincing romance, the plot is insufficiently intriguing to save the film. Most reviewers found the story lacking in depth and "oddly uninspired." A British critic called it "fundamentally flawed." Another reviewer stated, "Alas, this is pitiful stuff that never engages."

Nor was *Death Defying Acts* a box office success. With an extremely limited release in small U.S. markets, it grossed only about $6.5 million. Some have questioned why Weinstein bought the property, and why he then released it up against summer superhero blockbusters.

While most reviewers agreed that the film's core components (plot, leading performances, and direction) were weak, they also agreed that the movie's cinematography was its primary strength. Visually, *Death Defying Acts* is very appealing, "with loads of period flashes to absorb viewers in the movie's atmosphere." The underwater filming is particularly "gorgeous," and the shots of Houdini escaping from the water torture cell are genuinely dramatic. They are possibly more effectively shot here than in any other film about Houdini. The actual water cell prop is now on display at Davenport's Magic Kingdom in London.

Additionally, the majority of reviewers credit two supporting actors, Saoirse Ronan, as McGarvie's daughter, and Timothy Spall, as Houdini's manager, with strong performances. Ronan will be remembered for her sterling portrayal of Briony Tallis, the thirteen-year-old child whose false accusation changes the course of several lives in the film *Atonement* (2007). Spall, a seasoned character actor, delivers a charming portrayal of Houdini's manager, who faithfully endeavors to insulate Houdini from treachery and embarrassment.

The movie's performance of magical effects is quite minimal, despite the fact that Guy Pearce spent six weeks earnestly learning sleight of hand from magician Paul Skiffington. (Scott Penrose was the film's magic consultant.) *Death Defying Acts* is also disappointing in its failure to portray the extensive production elements of mounting a theatrical stage show by the world's most acclaimed magical master: there are no rehearsals, no scampering of assistants before showtime, no moving of large illusions to their marks. The electricity of show business is at no time felt in the film.

With its stellar cast and intriguing premise, *Death Defying Acts* had the potential to be an enchanting movie. But as one critic put it, the film is "a bit of a snore."

MOVIE CREDITS

Director	Gillian Armstrong
Magic Consultant	Scott Penrose
Original Screenplay	Tony Grisoni Brian Ward
Producers	Chris Curling Marian Macgowan
Production Company	Australian Film Finance Corporation Myriad Pictures
Featured Cast	Guy Pearce Catherine Zeta-Jones Timothy Spall Saoirse Ronan
Composer	Cezary Skubiszewski

Cinematographer	Haris Zambarloukos
Editor	Nicholas Beauman
Distributor	Third Rail Releasing
Film Festival Release date	September 13, 2007 (Toronto Film Festival)
U.S. (limited) Release date	July 11, 2008
DVD Release date	October 28, 2008
Running time	97 minutes
MPAA rating	PG
B/W or Color	Color
Where to Find?	*Death Defying Acts* is available for purchase from Amazon in DVD and Blu-ray formats.

For online viewing, the movie is available to rent or to buy from Amazon Video (in HD format), YouTube, Google Play, iTunes, and Vudu.

THE LAST MAGIC SHOW (2007)

*T*HE *L*AST *M*AGIC *S*HOW has been described as a modern-day fairy tale, told with a dreamlike flair. Whether or not the film belongs in this book depends on one's interpretation of events within the movie's enchanting plot. Does the leading character Ronny Roman (Andy Conlan) possess real magical powers, as he himself believes, or is this belief a matter of self-deception? The film's charm depends on neither conclusion, and the ambiguity is undoubtedly purposeful.

The Last Magic Show probes the tormented psyche of a young illusionist. Roman has been traumatized by finding his childhood sweetheart and assistant in the embrace of another magician. His retreat into a fantasy world quite clearly reflects his vulnerability and his fear of failure as a magician. His ultimate willingness to attempt an escape that puts him at risk of drowning and electrocution symbolizes his deliverance from this tortured state.

An independent New Zealand film with a budget of only $25,000, *The Last Magic Show* received enthusiastic reviews. The first feature film from writer, director, and actor Andy Conlan was praised, "There's a lot of wonderful weirdness to be had here, which makes for some great laughs and an enjoyable film."

The movie was shot on location throughout Auckland, North Shore, and Davenport, New Zealand, and its cinematographer Duncan Cole was honored by the 2007 New Zealand Screen Awards for Best Technical Contribution to a Digital Feature. The film additionally won the Honorable Mention Award at the Dances With Films Festival in Los Angeles.

The film's actors are all remarkably talented and believable, despite their exaggerated quirkiness. The characters range from maliciously creepy to delicately gentle, with Michael Hurst, as Roman's sleazy manager, and Georgie Hill, as a germophobic nurse, turning in brilliant performances.

With its special quality of sweetness and charm, this movie is definitely worth watching.

———

MOVIE CREDITS

Director	Andy Conlan
Original Screenplay	Andy Conlan
Producer	Andy Conlan
Production Companies (N.Z.)	The Best Fancy Magic Show Ever Tamarillo Films
Featured Cast	Andy Conlan Jade Collins Michael Hurst Matthew Sunderland Lucy Wigmore
Composer	Luke Fitzgerald
Cinematographer	Duncan Cole
Editor	Ahab Blin
U.S. Distributor	Arkles Entertainment
U.S. Release date	July 11, 2007

Running time	90 minutes
MPAA rating	NR
B/W or Color	Color
Where to Find?	*The Last Magic Show* is not available, at press time, for purchase from Amazon.
	However, for online viewing, one can access this New Zealand movie hub: http://www.flicks.co.nz/movie/the-last-magic-show/

IS ANYBODY THERE? (2008)

Edward (Bill Milner) is a ten-year-old boy who lives in a home for senior citizens that is run by his parents. With residents dying on a weekly basis, Edward becomes obsessed with ghosts and the afterlife. He becomes increasingly reclusive, until a curmudgeonly retired magician, "The Amazing Clarence" (Sir Michael Caine), begrudgingly takes up residence in the seaside home. Clarence is suffering from accelerating dementia, and he bitterly mourns the loss of his wife. He is delightfully spiteful, hostile, and unfriendly. Clarence develops a relationship with Edward that goes from loathing to love. As far as plots go, this one has some predictable elements, none of which, however, detract from the story's poignancy and delicate insights. The subtleties of the script and the brilliant chemistry of Caine and Milner result in a movie that quietly triumphs with its multiple messages.

Is Anybody There? is a British independent film written by Peter Harness, who drew upon his own experience growing up in a nursing home. It might appear that the used-up magician Clarence was a role written specifically for Caine, but when the director, John Crowley, agreed to do the project with Harness, it was only then they agreed Caine would be perfect for the part. Remarkably, Caine read the script and signed on without hesitation, although filming was delayed for eight months while Caine completed his work on *The Dark Knight* (2008). Caine was quoted as saying, "Many scripts make me laugh, but this one made me laugh, and it also made me cry. That hadn't happened before."

While portraying Clarence's personality traits was probably not difficult for an actor of Caine's caliber, crafting his persona as a magician may have been a bit more challenging. In recalling magicians who had performed at parties for his daughters, Caine noticed they all parted their hair in the middle, "[s]o, the first thing I did was part my hair in the middle." When he inquired of the film's magic consultant why magicians all seemed to have this coiffure, Scott Penrose replied, "Houdini parted his in the middle, and we are fans of Houdini."

As to understanding the process of dementia, Caine drew on his friendship with famous English tailor Doug Hayward, who was an inspiration to Caine when he was making the film *Alfie* in 1966. Hayward died of dementia while *Is Anybody There?* was being shot. Caine said that his wife cried when she saw the film, for reasons that are quite understandable.

While both Caine (a two-time Oscar winner) and Milner (who had appeared previously in a television movie, *Son of Rambow*, 2008) deserve enormous credit for the film's resonance, director Michael Crowley certainly must receive praise for the movie's success. In Britain, a background in theater seems to be a prerequisite for any film director, and Crowley had received a Tony Award nomination for Best Director in 2005 for *The Plowman*. Crowley's ability to engage an extraordinary supporting cast has been credited to his stage experience. As stated in the film's production notes:

> Crowley's theatre experience also benefitted the casting process. To play the residents of the retirement home, the filmmakers were able to assemble a who's-who of veteran British actors. Rosemary Harris [Elsie, in the film], a Tony Award-winning and Oscar-nominated actress, is well known to younger audiences as May Parker in the *Spiderman* trilogy. Leslie Phillips [Reg], whose voice is familiar to Harry Potter fans as that of the Sorting Hat, has worked extensively with London's Royal Shakespeare Company. Sylvia Syms has three BAFTA Award nominations and played the Queen Mother opposite Oscar winner Helen Mirren in Stephen Frears' acclaimed biopic *The Queen*. In fact, it's difficult to name an actor in the ensemble without a host of accolades and decades of work behind them.

While *Is Anybody There?* opened to extremely positive reviews, a small number of critics did not appreciate the film. For the most part, these reviewers were from the United States rather than Britain, and they seemed disinclined to embrace the genre. *NPR's* Bob Mondello found the movie "predictable and implausible." Other reviewers called the film "morbid" and "depressing," "maudlin," and "charmingly forgettable." But these reviews were in the minority, and the overwhelming majority of critics extended nothing but high praise, recognizing that, as John Walsh noted in the *Independent*, "It's the little details that lift Crowley's film from black humor into something warmer." In a similar vein, Bruce DeMara of the *Toronto Star* wrote, "There's a touch of magic at play here, but it is of the understated variety, delivering a finale that is unexpectedly hopeful, moving, and emotionally satisfying."

The film is best summed up by Philip Wilding on the Empire Online website, "Caine leads an impeccable cast in a story that is as touching as it is funny, turning the mundane of fading lives into a vibrant display."

MOVIE CREDITS

Director	John Crowley
Magic Consultant	Scott Penrose
Original Screenplay	Peter Harness
Producers	David Heyman Peter Saraf Marc Turtletub
Production Companies (U.K.)	BBC Films Heydey Films
Production Company (U.S.)	Big Beach Films

Featured Cast	Sir Michael Caine
	Bill Milner
	David Morrissey
	Anne-Marie Duff
Composer	Joby Talbot
Cinematographer	Rob Hardy
Editor	Trevor Waite
U.S. Distributor	Stony Island Entertainment
Film Festival Release date	September 7, 2008 (Toronto Film Festival)
U.S. Release date	May 15, 2009
Running time	94 minutes
MPAA rating	PG-13
B/W or Color	Color
Where to Find?	*Is Anybody There?* is available for purchase from Amazon in DVD and Blu-ray formats.
	For online viewing, the film is available to rent or to buy from Amazon Video (in SD format), iTunes, YouTube, Google Play, Vudu, and DVD.com.

THE GREAT
BUCK HOWARD (2008)

T HE AMAZING KRESKIN, born George Joseph Kresge Jr., is a self-declared mentalist who became a popular U.S. television personality because of his *The Amazing World of Kreskin* (which aired from 1970-1975) and *The New Kreskin Show* (which aired for the remainder of the decade). While the television shows were undoubtedly the crescendo of his career, Kreskin continues to enjoy the spotlight, though an ever-dimming one, even today.

Kreskin's act has consisted of a curious array of stunts and demonstrations including revealing the thoughts of audience members, predicting Super Bowl scores, and finding hidden objects. In a recurrent feature of his stage show, he asks to have the check for his performance hidden on the premises, coupled with the promise that if he fails to find it, he will forfeit his fee. Several sources agree that in performing this feat in thousands of acts, he has only failed nine times.

What is truly amazing about Kreskin is that he has taken a very limited number of stunts and presented them in such an entertaining fashion. He has made over five hundred television appearances, including ninety-eight on *The Merv Griffin Show*, one hundred eighteen on *The Mike Douglas Show*, dozens on *The Late Show with David Letterman*, several on *Late Night with Jimmy Fallon*, and more appearances on *The Tonight Show Starring Johnny Carson* than any other mentalist. He has also been a frequent radio guest on *The Howard Stern Show*. Even today in his eighties, he continues to perform his stage shows, although in smaller venues than during his earlier years.

Now an established Hollywood writer, Sean McGinly worked for Kreskin as a road manager at a time when Kreskin's light was beginning to dim. McGinly had dropped out of law school and was apparently eager to take any position that would connect him to the entertainment business. McGinly wrote a movie script about his experience with Kreskin, and years later, with Kreskin's blessing, McGinly's *The Great Buck Howard* debuted.

The character Buck Howard is brilliantly played by John Malkovich who uses exaggerated gestures and mood swings in what can only be seen as a caricature of the mentalist. As stated by Stephen Holden in the *New York Times*, "Kreskin's courtly geniality assumes a creepy edge of self-deluding egomania." But as Holden points out, despite its many satirical thrusts, the film "insists on being nice." Kreskin, in a video interview accompanying the DVD, seems to enjoy the attention the movie brings him; at minimum, it can be said that Kreskin is a very good sport. He very much appears to be a man who can laugh—if not guffaw—at himself.

Generally viewed as a charming indie film, *The Great Buck Howard* was praised for its nuanced insight into the arc of a performer's career. Malkovich, according to most reviewers, turned in a marvelously weird performance. Even when it was over-the-top, the performance had a certain strange believability.

Colin Hanks, in the role of Buck Howard's road manager Troy Gable, plays his part with the requisite restraint to counterbalance Malkovich's hyperbolic character. Moreover, Colin Hanks, the son of Tom Hanks, and best known for his role in *Orange County* (2002), was instrumental in bringing the project to the screen; he read the script in 2003 and "fell in love with it." He worked for months with the writer-director Sean McGinly, trying to find the financing for the project. In an interview with Steve Prokopy, Chicago editor for the *Ain't it Cool News* website, Colin Hanks said that he submitted the script to his father's production company, Playtime, for advice to "...help us [Hanks and McGinly] in the direction of somewhere we could go..." Tom Hanks and his partner Gary Goetzman liked the script and offered to take on the project. In the same interview, Colin Hanks also revealed that Kevin Kline originally agreed to play Buck Howard, but by the time financing was secured, Kline had made other commitments.

While Malkovich's ceaseless self-aggrandizing dominates the film, other cast members do excellent work in supporting roles. Emily Blunt is quirky, unpredictable, and perfectly irreverent as Valerie, a savvy New York publicist sent to promote a comeback event for Howard that involves putting hundreds of people into a trance. The stunt works, but the press corps leaves before the climax to cover an automobile accident involving Jerry Springer.

Debra Monk turns in a spot-on performance as a Cincinnati promoter who introduces Howard onstage with a rendition of The Lovin' Spoonful's "Do You Believe in Magic." There are cameos by Tom Hanks, as well as by Tom Arnold, Conan O'Brien, Jay Leno, Jon Stewart, Martha Stewart, David Blaine, Regis Philbin, Kelly Ripa, George Takei, and Mary Hart. Ricky Jay briefly appears as Howard's manager; Colin Hanks and Sean McGinly had hoped he would play a larger part, but his schedule did not permit it. Tony Clark served as the movie's magic consultant.

Buck Howard is not a great movie, or an important one, but it is very entertaining. As Kreskin himself said in an interview, "Usually you don't have a movie that's based on you unless you've committed serial killing, or have a Ponzi scheme behind you, or you have been dead for twenty years." And that is what makes *The Great Buck Howard* such an intriguing film.

MOVIE CREDITS

Director   Sean McGinly

Magic Consultant   Tony Clark

Original Screenplay   Sean McGinly

Producers   Gary Goetzman
                        Tom Hanks

Production Company   Playtone

Featured Cast	John Malkovich
	Colin Hanks
	Emily Blunt
	Tom Hanks
	Adam Scott
Composer	Blake Neely
Cinematographer	Tak Fujimoto
Editor	Myron I. Kerstein
Distributor	Magnolia Pictures
Film Festival Release date	January 18, 2008 (Sundance Film Festival)
U.S. Release date	April 10, 2009
Running time	90 minutes
MPAA rating	PG
B/W or Color	Color
Where to Find?	*The Great Buck Howard* is available for purchase from Amazon in DVD or Blu-ray formats.
	For online viewing, the movie is available to rent or to buy from iTunes, Google Play, YouTube, and Vudu.

THE ILLUSIONIST (2010)

*T*HE ILLUSIONIST is an incredibly beautiful animated film directed by Sylvain Chomet. It is based on an unproduced script by Jacques Tati, written in 1956. Tati is the iconic French comedian and director behind *Mon Oncle* (1958), *Playtime* (1967), and several other successful films. He was known for his minimalist use of dialogue and the creation of a film character, Mr. Hulot, a man who struggles with an ever-changing world.

The main character in *The Illusionist* is based on Tati himself. His name is Tatischaff, Tati's actual surname, and the character is artistically drawn to have Tati's appearance, complete with a stiff walk, an omnipresent raincoat, and sad, baggy eyes. There is even a moment in the film when Tatischaff goes to the movies to see *Mon Oncle* and encounters a real-life incarnation of himself on the screen.

The film's story follows an elderly magician as he goes from one gig to another. Along the journey, he is joined by a young teenage woman, Alice, an appreciative admirer. She brightens the illusionist's loneliness and despair over the dying nature of his career. As for the girl, she has an opportunity to escape her destiny as a server and floor mopper in a small pub.

The film carefully avoids any suggestion of a romance between the illusionist and Alice, making their relationship one of father and daughter. While Alice remains relatively young, the connection between the two characters works well. Of course, time changes everything, and the film concludes with inevitable sadness and yearning. The film, however, should not be called despairing. As Scott Tobias of *NPR* insightfully points out, the film does foster a belief in magic—not the kind that materializes out of thin air, but in those small, crucial moments of generosity and connection that enrich our lives.

The Illusionist premiered to rave reviews at the 2010 Berlin International Film Festival and has been praised for its many remarkable attributes. *Rotten Tomatoes* gave *The Illusionist* a score of 90% percent based on the reviews of one hundred fourteen critics, calling the film an "engrossing love letter to fans of adult animation. *The Illusionist* offers a fine antidote to garish mainstream fare." Roger Ebert gave the film four out of four stars. The film was nominated at the 68th Golden Globe Awards for Best Animated Feature Film, and it was nominated for Best Animated Feature Film in the 83rd Academy Awards, but lost both to *Toy Story 3* (2010).

Sylvain Chomet's style of animation, first introduced in *The Triplets of Belleville* (2003), is enchanting and known for its gorgeous detail. There is not a computer-generated image in *The Illusionist*. The hand-drawn panoramas of Paris, Edinburgh, and the coastal areas of Scotland are like museum-quality watercolors. Apart from its poignant story, the film's sheer visual beauty is unforgettable. Peter Bradshaw in the *Guardian* noted, "Simply being an animation, an old-style animation, is a great effect. *The Illusionist* is like a séance that brings to life scenes from the 1950s with eerie directness in a way that glitzy digital animation or live-action period location work could somehow never do."

Tati's original script played a unique role in the making of this film. Written in 1956, it was closely guarded by Tati's family. It has been suggested that the film may have been too personally painful for Tati to produce. The story is autobiographically a tribute to one of Tati's daughters. Tati's daughter, Sophie, gave the script to Chomet, and Chomet has steadfastly confirmed that the story was about Tati and Sophie. But the family of Tati's abandoned illegitimate daughter, Helga Marie-Jeanne Schiel, believes that she is the film's true inspiration, and they have called for Chomet to publicly acknowledge Schiel's role in Tati's life and the film. The conflict has never been resolved, but appreciating that the film is inspired by a man's relationship with a daughter who matures and believes less and less in her father's magic does help immensely in understanding the heartbreaking transcendence of the film.

Movie Credits

Director	Sylvain Chomet
Original Screenplay	Jacque Tati
Adapted Screenplay	Sylvain Chomet
Producers	Sally Chomet Bob Last
Production Companies (France)	Pathé Ciné B France 3 Cinéma
Production Company (U.K.)	Django Films
Featured Cast (Voices)	Jean-Claude Donda Eilidh Rankin Duncan MacNeil
Composer	Sylvain Chomet
Art Director (Animation)	Bjarne Hansen
Editor	Sylvain Chomet
U.S. Distributor	Sony Pictures Classics
Film Festival Release date	September 5, 2010 (Telluride Film Festival)

U.S. Release date   February 11, 2011

Running time   80 minutes

MPAA rating   PG

B/W or Color   Color

Where to Find?   *The Illusionist* is available for purchase from Amazon in DVD and Blu-ray formats, and in a "Two-Disc Blue-ray/DVD Combo" set.

For online viewing, the film is available to rent or to buy from Amazon Video (in SD/HD formats), Google Play, iTunes, YouTube, and Vudu.

HUGO (2011)

MARTIN SCORSESE is considered by many to be the most respect-ed director of all time. Primarily known for critically acclaimed R-rated films about the underbelly of major American cities—*Mean Streets* (1973), *Taxi Driver* (1976), *Raging Bull* (1980), *Goodfellas* (1990), *Casino* (1995), *Gangs of New York* (2002), and *The Departed* (2006)—his lighter films have been considered less successful than his darker movies. Many were also box office failures—e.g., *New York, New York* (1977) and *The King of Comedy* (1983).

Hugo, however, is unlike any other Scorsese film. Receiving almost unanimous critical acclaim, *Hugo* is a family movie that is richly enchant-ing and marvelously entertaining. Based on the intriguing book *The Invention of Hugo Cabret* by Brian Selznick (a cousin of David O. Selznick, producer of *Gone with the Wind*), the story is a historical adventure, perhaps best understood as a fable. The plot is exceptionally original, even though it is constructed around the real-life character of Georges Méliès, the great film pioneer.

The movie is set in Paris in 1931, and its primary character, Hugo (Asa Butterfield), is an orphan living in the secret walls and chambers of the Gare Montparnasse railway station. He lives with his alcoholic uncle, who is charged with keeping all the station's clocks running. When his uncle disappears, Hugo maintains the task of keeping the clock machin-ery operational. If the clocks were to stop, his uncle's absence would be noticed, and Hugo would be taken to an orphanage, a fate he ardently seeks to avoid.

Hugo remains connected to his deceased father by an automaton in need of missing mechanical parts to make it operate. Hugo's quest for those parts, as well as for a critical key that would turn on the automaton, leads him on a hunt through the railway station. He is repeatedly chased by the vindictive station inspector, comically played by Sacha Baron Cohen. Living as a phantom in the shadowland of the station, Hugo manages to scavenge all the parts for the automaton except the secret key.

Amid plot twists that involve his barely escaping apprehension, Hugo encounters a shopkeeper, touchingly played by Ben Kingsley, who sells mechanical toys in the station. He also meets the self-assured Isabelle (Chloë Grace Moretz), a girl of Hugo's age, and the shopkeeper's goddaughter. Again, the plot twirls fascinatingly, ultimately revealing that the shopkeeper is Georges Méliès, who has abandoned his career as the renowned creator of some of the earliest films produced for entertainment.

Hugo warrants a place in this book because Georges Méliès began his career as a stage magician. In 1888, Méliès' father retired from his prosperous shoe business and ceded it to his three sons. Georges sold his share to his brothers, which enabled him to acquire the Theatre Robert-Houdin in Paris to create a venue for his passion for magic. According to Erik Barnouw in his book *The Magician and the Cinema* (1981), Georges had become an infatuated habitué of Egyptian Hall while spending time in London training for the family shoe business. Egyptian Hall, "England's Home of Mystery," was founded in 1813 by John Nevil Maskelyne and Georges Alfred Cooke to house a theater showcasing their magical inventions. Both Egyptian Hall and Paris' Theatre Robert-Houdin originally served as venues for magical performances and later became theaters for the debut of cinema.

After a brief struggle to acquire the proper mechanical equipment, Méliès collaborated with London inventor Robert W. Paul, enabling Méliès to plunge into a career of filmmaking that would result in approximately five hundred films. Perhaps his most famous film is the 1902 movie *Journey to the Moon*, which contains the iconic image of the man in the moon with a rocket piercing his eye.

By the mid-1920s, magic theaters were replaced by movie theaters, as the mystery of early moving-picture projections was replaced by a public appetite for longer, more serious, more romantic films. As interest in short films featuring the fantastic, the grotesque, and the impossible faded, motion pictures became arenas for major corporations, not individual artisans. Méliès made no films after 1913, and the shuttering of theaters at the beginning of World War I contributed to Méliès' financial decline.

The film *Hugo* finds Méliès in his later years, occupying a kiosk in the Gare Montparnasse, and Scorsese's images are drawn from authentic photographs of Méliès' small shop contained in New York's Museum of Modern Art. Here history and storytelling intertwine as the movie chronicles the young boy Hugo scavenging parts for the automaton during a period of world interest in the films of Georges Méliès, many of which are authentically presented in *Hugo*.

Hugo won five Oscars: Best Cinematography, Best Art Direction, Best Visual Effects, Best Sound Mixing, and Best Sound Editing. It received the largest number of nominations—eleven total, including Best Picture and Best Director. Scorsese received his third Golden Globe Award for Best Director. He received critical acclaim for his masterful use of 3-D, and *Rotten Tomatoes* gave the film a 94% rating on its Tomato Meter. Peter Travers in *Rolling Stone* praised the film, "*Hugo* will take your breath away. It truly is stuff that dreams are made of." According to Daniel Dewey of the *New Yorker*:

> The emotional pull of the story is irresistible. The boy needs a family, the illustrious filmmaker needs to regain his past, and a love of movies brings them together. Reality, filmed illusion, and dreams are so intertwined that only an artist playing merrily with echoes can sort them into a scheme of delight.

Roger Ebert of the *Chicago Sun Times* gave the film four out of four stars. It was selected by Richard Corliss of *Time* as one of the Top 10 Best Movies of 2011. While the film did receive a smattering of negative reviews, most notably in the *Wall Street Journal*, these critiques appear to misunderstand the movie and are eclipsed by the near-unanimous acclaim it otherwise received.

Hugo is unquestionably a grand film, and a monumental contribution in connecting magic as a performing art to the origins of cinema.

MOVIE CREDITS

Director	Martin Scorsese
Based upon	Brian Selznick's novel *The Invention of Hugo Cabret* (2007)
Screenplay	John Logan
Producers	Johnny Depp Tim Headington Graham King Martin Scorsese
Production Companies	Infinitum Nihil GK Films
Featured Cast	Ben Kingsley Sacha Baron Cohen Asa Butterfield Chloë Grace Moretz Ray Winstone Christopher Lee Jude Law
Composer	Howard Shore
Cinematographer	Robert Richardson
Editor	Thelma Schoonmaker
Distributor	Paramount Pictures

Film Festival Release date	October 10, 2011 (New York Film Festival)
U.S. Release date	November 23, 2011
Running time	126 minutes
MPAA rating	PG
B/W or Color	Color
Where to Find?	*Hugo* is available for purchase from Amazon in DVD and Blue-ray formats (including a 3D Blu-ray edition).
	For online viewing, the film is available to rent or to buy from Amazon Video (in HD format), iTunes, YouTube, Google Play, and Vudu.

THE INCREDIBLE
BURT WONDERSTONE (2013)

S TEVE CARELL, as the title character Burt Wonderstone, is an arrogant magician who falls out of favor when his partner, Anton Marvelton (Steve Buscemi), leaves their act. Wonderstone attempts to go it alone, but his efforts are complicated by a popular new performer named Steve Gray (Jim Carrey). Wonderstone's subsequent effort to save his career and find recognition as a decent human being is formulaic and only occasionally funny. With a stellar cast that includes Olivia Wilde, Alan Arkin, and James Gandolfini, *The Incredible Burt Wonderstone* was predicted to be a huge success. Unfortunately, the film drew disappointing box office receipts and mixed reviews.

Development of *Wonderstone* began in 2006 when New Line Cinema acquired a script, "Burt Dickerson: The Most Powerful Magician on Planet Earth." John Francis Daley and Jonathan Goldstein reworked the screenplay, which was then subsequently rewritten by (uncredited) Jason Reitman. Some critics cited this "writing-by-committee" as the reason the movie failed to be a smash hit, despite the powerhouse comedic cast. In an interview with Daley and Goldstein, who wrote the very funny film *Horrible Bosses* (2011), the writers stated that the script went through numerous changes, including fifteen drafts over a three-and-a-half-year period. According to producer Chris Bender:

> It was tone, finding the right tone, because it was originally written more broadly where certain magic things were happening that wouldn't actually be real magic, and also over time the references that we were making in terms of the new school of magic and the

old school of magic were becoming dated….Once [Carell] came on board, that's when things really took off….And then finding the right director, too. These kinds of comedies scare directors a lot, because you're taking a chance, and you're going for something bold comedy-wise that either could be a big hit or it could really miss.

Wonderstone was directed by television veteran Don Scardino, who is known for his work on *30 Rock*. Scardino made further changes to the script after he joined the project by deleting magic tricks that could never be performed by mortal magicians. Wanting to make the film more believable, he insisted that the film's illusions must be actually accomplishable. David Copperfield served as the primary technical consultant and created a featured illusion involving a hangman and body switch expressly for the film, and he also made a cameo appearance. The Misdirectors Guild, a consulting group of magicians, worked closely with Scardino to ensure the authenticity of the illusions.

Veteran stunt coordinator Alex Daniels masterfully supervised such stunts as the "hot box" scene, which was filmed on location in front of Bally's with dozens of spectators looking on. The scene showed Wonderstone and Anton attempting a survivalist stunt in a glass box suspended fifty feet in the air by a crane. Daniels stated in an interview with the *Las Vegas Blog*:

> One of the reasons the hot box sequence in *The Incredible Burt Wonderstone* got so much buzz was that so many people in Las Vegas at the time got to see the scene being shot. The other thing that was unique about it was we were able to get great reactions from people on the Strip. Not just our extras, but spectators. They could watch the comedic flow and respond to the sequence in a genuine, visceral way.

It is no surprise that stunt doubles were used for the more dangerous shots. Daniels explained:

Both actors were in the box when we lifted them up to the highest point, about fifty feet up. From another crane, we were able to get some great shots of the box and the actors and the people on the Strip. Once we got into the more stunt-oriented part of the sequence, where the box is open and the people are hanging, the stunt team stepped in.

Other scenes were filmed on location as well. Director Scardino used locations like Bally's, the Las Vegas Strip, downtown Las Vegas, Fremont Street, and Binion's Gambling Hall to give the film authenticity. Around four hundred extras played pedestrians, tourists, and casino employees. Carell and Carrey were filmed in several scenes on location.

While *Wonderstone* failed to live up to its anticipated blockbuster status, it is not without its bright spots. Jim Carrey was uniformly praised for what Ann Hornaday of the *Washington Post* described as "a magnificently deranged job of skewering the insane hijinks of such performers as David Blaine and Criss Angel." As Steve Gray, Carrey has a television show called *The Brain Rapist*. Carrey went on a strict diet to improve his physique for the role, which has him doing such things as pounding a nail into a table with his forehead.

Supporting cast members were also credited for turning fine but script-limited performances. As a casino owner, James Gandolfini is well cast. Michael Phillips of the *Chicago Tribune* praised Alan Arkin's performance: "The actor can't save the movie, but he can save his scenes." Richard Roeper agreed, "As the crusty, slightly insane old-schooler with a few tricks up his sleeve, Arkin is a marvel." Dana Stevens, on *Slate's* website, described Olivia Wilde's performance as the mistreated magician's assistant as "likeable but under-challenged."

Despite its shortcomings, *The Incredible Burt Wonderstone* is a must-see for anyone interested in the contemporary magic scene. If nothing else, the film demonstrates how difficult it is to imagine a stereotypical magician, and how challenging it must be for any performing magician to create a crowd-pleasing persona.

MOVIE CREDITS

Director	Don Scardino
Magic Consultants	David Copperfield
	David Kwong
	Jonathan Levitt
	Homer Liwag
	Chris Kenner
Story by	Chad Kultgen
	Tyler Mitchell
	Jonathan Goldstein
	John Francis Daley
Screenplay	Jonathan Goldstein
	John Francis Daley
Producers	Chris Bender
	Steve Carell
	Tyler Mitchell
	Jake Weiner
Production Companies	New Line Cinema
	Benderspink
	Carousel
Featured Cast	Steve Carell
	Steve Buscemi
	Olivia Wilde
	Alan Arkin
	James Gandolfini
	Jim Carrey

Composer	Lyle Workman
Cinematographer	Matthew Clark
Editor	Lee Haxall
Distributor	Warner Bros. Pictures
Film Festival Release date	March 8, 2013 (SxSW Film Festival)
U.S. Release date	March 15, 2013
Running time	100 minutes
MPAA rating	PG-13
B/W or Color	Color
Where to Find?	*The Incredible Burt Wonderstone* is available for purchase from Amazon in DVD and Blue-ray formats. For online viewing, the movie is available to rent or to buy from Amazon Video (in HD format), iTunes, YouTube, Google Play, Vudu, and DVD.com.

NOW YOU SEE ME (2013)

FOUR MAGICIANS—J. Daniel Atlas (Jesse Eisenberg), a sleight of hand artist; Merritt McKinney (Woody Harrelson), a mentalist; Henley Reeves (Ilsa Fisher), an escape artist; and Jack Wilder (Dave Franco), a street magician—are brought together by an unknown benefactor to create a grand-scale Las Vegas act that becomes known as "The Four Horsemen." Later, we discover that the producer of the act is insurance magnate Arthur Tressler (Sir Michael Caine).

A year later, playing before a packed house in a Las Vegas hotel, The Four Horsemen declare they will rob a bank in Paris. Through the apparent teleportation of a member of the audience holding an account at the Crédit Républicain de Paris, the audience member suddenly disappears and reappears in the bank's vault, all seen on a Jumbotron. A vacuum in the air duct of the French bank vault transports the money to the Las Vegas showroom where it is showered on the audience—creating a massive bank heist by magic. FBI Agent Dylan Rhodes (Mark Ruffalo) is assigned to investigate the case, and he is joined by Interpol Agent Alma Dray (Mélanie Laurent) in his efforts. The primary cast is complete when Rhodes meets Thaddeus Bradley (Morgan Freeman), a master at explaining the workings of tricks and illusions on television specials. He offers to assist Rhodes in bringing The Four Horsemen to justice.

The cast is brilliant, and the premise of magic as a means of committing larceny is compelling, but most critics failed to provide a favorable review of *Now You See Me*. The plot has been described as "ever-escalating ridiculous" and "ultimately silly and substandard." While some reviewers found individual segments entertaining and spectacular, the film was described by Matt Neal in the *Standard* "…as a bunch of really cool tricks that are enjoyable so you won't notice that there is no depth, no emotion, no themes, and no character development." The story involves a "master plan" depending on so many variables that could go wrong that the plot seems contrived at best, absurd at worst.

A few reviewers did like the film and praised the acting and the plot as engaging. But the biggest supporters of the film were the ticket-buying audiences, who responded to the movie with an incredible $350 million in box office receipts. The film was so popular that a sequel was shot in 2015, with most of the cast reprising their roles.* Not taking the film as seriously as movie critics did, the movie-going public appears to like the gratifying Robin Hood theme that threads throughout the film, as well as the sheer momentum of the story.

Some of the misconceptions about the film center on the issue of whether or not The Four Horsemen use supernatural powers to perform their illusions. Some reviewers were critical of the film because in cinema, the laws of physics and scientific principles are irrelevant. Any magic trick or illusion is possible, no matter how outlandish. Consequently, the spectacular nature of The Four Horsemen's illusions is no different than the special effects that have become commonplace in a substantial segment of the movie industry.

But seeing The Horsemen's illusions as mere "special effects" dismisses the genuine performances of magic in the film. Director Louis Leterrier engaged David Kwong and his company the Misdirectors Guild, to serve not simply as the film's magic consultants, but also to actually help create the movie's three major magical performances. Every illusion was designed to be possible without special effects. "They [the Horsemen] never do anything that is supernatural. These are real human beings," said Kwong in an interview with Bryan Bishop on the *Verge* website. "When the actors surreptitiously palm and swap objects in one sequence, it was done live. Jesse Eisenberg does a great snap change of the card, which is in the trailer. He practiced forever.... Dave Franco, that guy just practiced throwing cards until he was better than anyone I have ever met."

It was so important to the film's plot that the magic be authentically possible that each major magical scene is deconstructed as part of the

---

* The sequel, *Now You See Me 2* (Summit Entertainment, 2016), is not included in this book because several of the magical effects depicted therein defy the laws of physics. *See, e.g.*, Michael O'Sullivan, "More of the same in 'Now You See Me 2'–for better or for worse," the *Washington Post*, June 9, 2016.

story. Yes, there are some extraordinary coincidences, but no rules of the universe are bent or broken. Failing to understand this critical fulcrum would make viewing the film a completely distorted experience.

———

MOVIE CREDITS

Director	Louis Leterrier
Head Magic Consultant	David Kwong
Story by	Boaz Yakin Edward Ricourt
Screenplay	Ed Solomon Boaz Yakin Edward Ricourt
Producers	Bobby Cohen Alex Kurtzman Roberto Orci
Production Company	K/O Paper Products
Featured Cast	Jesse Eisenberg Common Mark Ruffalo Woody Harrelson Isla Fisher Dave Franco Mélanie Laurent Sir Michael Caine Morgan Freeman

Composer	Brian Tyler
Cinematographers	Mitchell Amundsen Larry Fong
Editors	Robert Leighton Vincent Tabaillon
Distributor	Summit Entertainment
U.S. Release date	May 31, 2013
Running time	115 minutes
MPAA rating	PG-13
B/W or Color	Color
Where to Find?	*Now You See Me* is available for purchase from Amazon in DVD and Blu-ray formats. For online viewing, the movie is available to rent or to buy from Amazon Video (in HD format), iTunes, YouTube, Google Play, and Vudu.

MAGIC IN THE MOONLIGHT (2014)

IN AN INTERVIEW with Nigel M. Smith on the *Indiewire* website, Woody Allen stated, "I was an amateur magician as a boy. I loved everything about magic, and I did know in the history of magic that Houdini was somebody who would debunk spirit mediums who took advantage of people and took their money and preyed upon them." With this inspiration, Allen, the writer and director of *Magic in the Moonlight*, creates a love affair between a sophisticated, rationalist magician (Colin Firth) and a scam-artist spiritualist (Emma Stone). The plot is clever, the cast is excellent, and the film has a visual quality rarely seen in contemporary movies.

Allen's boyhood hobby—spending hours every day practicing sleight of hand tricks with billiard balls, cards, coins, and rings—has had an influence on a number of his films: *New York Stories* (1989), *The Curse of the Jade Scorpion* (2001), *Scoop* (2006), and *You Will Meet a Tall Dark Stranger* (2010), as well as *Magic in the Moonlight*. More charming than laugh-out-loud funny, Allen's *Magic* has been described as his "most exquisite-looking film in quite a while." Shot in the picturesque south of France, renowned cinematographer Darius Khondji used old Cinemascope lenses with 35mm. film to achieve a soft, luxurious, buttery hue. As stated by David Denby in the *New Yorker*, the elegance and luxury are "held in place by Allen's instructive classicism: the camera that gently recedes as the actors walk toward it, the long-lasting, immovable shots as people talk and talk. It's an accomplished, stately movie, unimpassioned but pleasing."

For some reviewers, such as Rex Reed in the *New York Observer*, *Magic in the Moonlight* is "near perfect," "...[a] master stroke of enchantment from one of the few comic geniuses of the modern cinema."

Several critics found Firth and Stone's performances to be "beyond perfect." Scott Foundas in *Variety* wrote, "[I]t's Stone's wonderful comic performance that shines brightest. Casting her hands before her as she communes with the spirit world and sounding astonished by the most mundane of revelations, her Sophie is the aloof dingbat original Shelly Duvall or Julie Hagerty used to play." Tom Shone in the *Guardian* said of Firth, "[H]e's like a mixture of Mr. Darcy and Henry Higgins….No other actor could have made it from skepticism to lyricism and back with quite the economy Firth manages here." David Denby in the *New Yorker* also praised Firth, writing, "The haughty reserve, the perfectly phrased disdain, the deeply romantic nature hidden beneath the chill. Firth does this sort of thing better than anyone." It is a draw as to whether Stone or Firth received the better reviews, and Scott Foundas in *Variety* praised both, "Whenever Firth and Stone are on screen together, the movie sings."

Woody Allen has made over forty-seven feature films. He has been nominated for twenty-four Academy Awards and has won four times. He has received more screenwriting Academy Award nominations than any other writer. At this point in his career, Allen has become a filmmaker who competes with himself. While a few critics have opined that *Magic* is not Allen's best film, most reviewers found something to like about the movie. Still, *Rotten Tomatoes* stated, "While far from a failure, *Magic in the Moonlight* is too light to stand with Woody Allen's finest work."

In addition to a superb cast and a clever plot, *Magic in the Moonlight* is a delight for the senses. Set in 1928, it captures the beauty of the Côte d'Azur. Accompanied by the romantic tunes of Jerome Kern, Cole Porter, and Rodgers and Hart, virtually everything sublime about this period is depicted: smart cars, formal balls, luscious suits, and gracious manners. The visual experience alone makes this film worth seeing.

Finally, Peter Travers in *Rolling Stone* made the following observation regarding the search for a refuge from the dull reality of life, "Is love the answer? Or is love too volatile to trust? Melancholy and doubt may seem like gloomy qualities to blend into an amorous romp. But that shot of gravity is what makes *Magic in the Moonlight* memorable and distinctly Woody Allen."

MOVIE CREDITS

Director	Woody Allen
Original Screenplay	Woody Allen
Producers	Letty Aronson Stephen Tenenbaum Edward Walson
Production Companies	Dippermouth Perido Productions Ske-Dat-De-Dat Productions
Featured Cast	Colin Firth Emma Stone Marcia Gay Harden Hamish Linklater Simon McBurney Jacki Weaver Eileen Atkins
Music Supervisor	Bobby Collins
Cinematographer	Darius Khondji
Editor	Alisa Lepselter
Distributor	Sony Pictures Classics
Film Festival Release date	August 3, 2014 (Traverse City Film Festival)

U.S. Release date	August 15, 2015
Running time	97 minutes
MPAA rating	PG-13
B/W or Color	Color
Where to Find?	*Magic in the Moonlight* is available for purchase from Amazon in DVD and Blue-ray formats.
	For online viewing, the film is available to rent or to buy from Amazon Video (in HD format), iTunes, YouTube, Google Play, and Vudu.

CONCLUSION

I T IS REMARKABLE that of the thousands of films made, and the hundreds that feature magic, only twenty-six contain plots in which the magician is a mere mortal devoid of any supernatural powers. One can only guess why the number is so small.

Perhaps magicians as human characters are not immediately perceived as interesting—at least not as interesting as private detectives, murderers, or lost souls looking for love. More likely, it is because magicians are simply obscure figures and are somewhat inaccessible to those who are not magicians themselves—or to those who do not generally contemplate the elements of mystery. Woody Allen, who has directed several films involving magicians, is both a practicing magician and a notably complex man. It appears that a director or writer must understand not only the skill of genuine magicians but also their philosophical bents to develop an interesting and entertaining film about magic.

Today, the most likely explanation for the dearth of movies about gifted mortal magicians is that cinematic techniques and special effects provide too great a temptation for film writers to create fantasies rather than to craft stories that could occur in reality.

Whatever the reason for the small number of films that realistically portray magicians, this book has endeavored to identify those movies for lovers of the true art and science of magic.

AUTHOR'S NOTE

AFTER DECADES OF WRITING for attorneys, judges, and law students, I am delighted to be pursuing a new phase of my career writing nonfiction books on popular culture, as well as novels.

Reel Magicians holds a special place in my heart. I have been fascinated with magic since the age of eight, when I received a Gilbert's Mysto Magic Show Set as a Christmas present. I was living on Long Island at the time and well remember the thrill of accompanying my father into Manhattan to explore Lou Tannen's Magic shop—with a ten-dollar budget for new tricks! As a teenager, I joined the local chapter of the International Brotherhood of Magicians and soon was performing professionally for birthday parties and similar events, honing my skills through my college years.

When my children became old enough to appreciate magic, my passion was revived. I served on the board of trustees for the International Brotherhood of Magicians (and as its Legal Counsel) under the presidencies of Ken Klosterman and Bev Bergeron. I edited *The Protection of Magicians' Secrets* (World Alliance of Magicians, Inc., 2000), which provides a comprehensive review of legal safeguards for magicians and their tricks, and served as chairman of World Alliance of Magicians, Inc.'s legal advisory committee. During this period, I also served as the chairman of the board of trustees for the Greater Cincinnati and Northern Kentucky Film Commission and taught graduate-level courses in film. The idea of writing a book marrying my love of magic and film took incipient form.

When I perform magic today, it is in a studio in my home that is devoted exclusively to parlor magic, its walls appointed with framed original posters for many of the movies I review in this book. Over the years,

I have acquired an extensive collection of magic paraphernalia, and my shows today include such well-known effects as cutting a woman in half and levitating a member of the audience in thin air.

I genuinely hope that you enjoyed *Reel Magicians*, and find it a valuable resource as you seek out films that capture the art, the science, and the mystery of magic. If you would be so kind as to leave a brief review of *Reel Magicians*, I would be very grateful; "word-of-mouth" support by means of reviews is vital for the success of any book. Merely a sentence or two of a review on Amazon would be tremendously appreciated.

Last, I am in the process of building The Weissenberger Artistic Alliance, at www.weissenbergerartisticalliance.com. Proceeds of the sales of *Reel Magicians* and my novels (see Appendix I and Appendix II), are directed to the Alliance, conceived as "A Creative Cultural Consortium for Charitable and Developing Artist Support." Our goal is to become a vibrant, interactive hub that both showcases and provides tangible support for multi-disciplinary, socially-conscious artists of all kinds—including magicians and performers in its allied arts. The Alliance affords educational opportunities (such as workshop and training stipends) to those emerging creative voices who share its goals of using various expressions of art to better society—to entertain us, to educate us, and to make us reflect.

I would love to hear from you! Please connect with me on LinkedIn, where I am co-administrator of its largest group for amateur and professional magicians ("Magicians, Mentalists, Hypnotists & Variety Entertainers"), as well as at the Alliance (glen@weissenbergerartisticalliance.com) in order that I can send you updates on release dates of my books, my scheduled media events, submission opportunities for artist education, and the like.

Thank you again for your support!

Glen Weissenberger

On Facebook: "Glen Weissenberger—The Weissenberger Artistic Alliance"

On Twitter: @weissenbergerjd and @TWArtAlliance
                @reelmagicians
                @made2measureman
                @companionsbykt

On LinkedIn, Goodreads, and Medium: "Glen Weissenberger"

FEATURED BONUS!
WOODY ALLEN'S
THE FLOATING LIGHT BULB
ON BROADWAY

Mr. Weissenberger would like to thank Gay Blackstone, Robert Aberdeen, and Brian Backer for making themselves available to be interviewed for this article.

I N THE EARLY 1980s, two Broadway productions featured the "Floating Lightbulb," a grand illusion originally created by Harry Blackstone Sr. Remarkably, these two shows ran within a few months of one another, with *The Magnificent Musical Magic Show* opening in May of 1980 and the play, *The Floating Light Bulb*, opening in April of 1981. The connection between these two productions appears undeniable.

According to Harry Blackstone Jr.:

The effect of defying gravity and floating an object in the air is one of the most beautiful effects in magic, but good things do not always come easily, and a really good levitation is one of the most difficult technical challenges there is in the profession.

In the early twentieth century, Harry Blackstone Sr. dazzled audiences by floating a glass of milk. It may not have been considered as spectacular as John Nevil Maskelyne's "Floating Princess Karnac," but it also did not require a permanent venue for its performance. While Princess Karnac was performed only in St. George's Hall—Maskelyne's permanent theater in London—the floating glass of milk was performed before thousands of people in countless venues both in the United States and abroad.

With the advent of widespread electricity, Blackstone Sr. collaborated with Thomas Alva Edison to create the "Floating Lightbulb." Considered by magicians and audiences alike to be one of the most baffling effects, the floating lightbulb is actually quite beautiful in its simplicity. After the bulb is removed from its electrical lamp, it remains illuminated, and it floats around the stage. After passing a hoop over the bulb several times, the magician says, "Oh, would you like to see it up close? All right, if you promise not to touch it, I'll let you look at it." At that moment, the bulb floats off the stage and stops inches in front of an audience member's face.

Today Blackstone Sr.'s and Edison's original floating lightbulb resides in the Smithsonian Museum, a gift from Harry Blackstone Jr. It was the first magical illusion acquired by the Smithsonian.

While initially Blackstone Jr. did not aspire to be a magician, his friend Tom Smothers (of the Smothers Brothers duo), convinced him to take over his father's show following Blackstone Sr.'s death in 1965. Blackstone Jr. thereafter toured the United States extensively, and his *Magnificent Musical Magic Show* opened on Broadway in May of 1980, where it ran for one hundred eighteen performances. The floating lightbulb was featured in each performance, along with many other famous Blackstone Sr. illusions such as the "Buzz Saw" (a savage-looking device to cut women in half) and the "Dancing Handkerchief."

According to Blackstone Jr's widow and assistant, Gay Blackstone, during the *Magnificent Musical Magic Show* run, ushers were quick to pass the word to him when celebrities were in the audience. Woody Allen was one such celebrity.

Woody Allen has often said he loves magic. He revealed in March 2015's *Genii* magazine, "As a kid I loved magic and might have become a magician if I hadn't been sidetracked." Roger Friedman in the *New York Observer* quoted Allen, "I bought tricks. I was interested in sleight of hand. I always read a lot about magic. I would do the tricks, stick a cigarette in my mother's silk handkerchief. It wouldn't work. The guys who do it are constantly practicing." Probably, Allen understated his skills. He auditioned at least twice as a teenager for television spots doing sophisticated magic effects. Indeed, in Allen and Stig Bjorkman's *Woody Allen on Woody Allen* (2005), Allen states, "Yes, I can still do it [magic]. I practiced it many days, many years. And I can still do all kinds of card manipulations and tricks with coins and similar things."

According to one his biographers, Eric Lax (*Conversations with Woody Allen*, 2009), Allen received a magic set when he was ten years old and was "thunderstruck." Allen stated, "I loved everything about it: the concept, the Chinese tissue papers, and the little cards with the fake backs to them, everything." Lax pointed out that Allen's passion for magic may not be well understood:

> My interest is its obvious symbolism, but it's fun to those who think it's fun. Someone like Mia [Farrow] or Diane Keaton, for example, cannot see it. It couldn't be more boring, [but] if you're hooked on it, you're hooked on it, and I was just completely, absolutely. I had a big drawer and it was full of magic tricks and I had these books [e.g. Ottoka Fischer's *Illustrated Magic* (1929)], and that was almost all I cared about.

It is not surprising that many of Allen's films, including the recent *Magic in the Moonlight*, involve magicians.

Within a few months of Blackstone Jr.'s *Magnificent Musical Magic Show*'s closing, Woody Allen's third Broadway play, *The Floating Light Bulb*, opened on April 27, 1981 at Lincoln Center's Vivian Beaumont Theater. Allen was already an acclaimed writer and actor with such film successes such as *Annie Hall* (1977) and *Manhattan* (1979) behind him. Additionally, his two previous Broadway plays, *Don't Drink the Water* (1966) and *Play It Again, Sam* (1969), had been commercial and critical successes: *Don't Drink the Water* ran for close to six hundred performances, and *Play It Again Sam*, starring Allen and Diane Keaton, earned three Tony Award nominations.

Surprising to some, *The Floating Light Bulb* received mixed reviews and closed after only sixty-two performances. Frank Rich, theater critic for the *New York Times*, noted that "*Light Bulb* is nothing to be embarrassed about, especially in the skilled direction by Ulu Grosbard,...but it would be easily mistaken for a journeyman effort by a much younger and less experienced writer."

Light Bulb's short run has been mistaken as a reflection of the play's lack of popularity. In fact, however, Allen had agreed to write a play for Lincoln Center's repertory season; by design, the play was slated for a limited run. Moreover, Robert Aberdeen, the magical consultant for *Light Bulb*, recalls that Allen had adapted the play from a short story he had previously written, and he valued it more for its artistic merit than its commercial potential. Indeed, according to Brian Backer, the actor who played the central character in the play, *Light Bulb* was actually held over for a week.

Film critics who expected *Light Bulb* to bear similarities to Allen's previous plays *Don't Drink the Water* or *Play It Again, Sam* would be inevitably disappointed, for those plays were specifically designed to reflect Allen's persona as an actor. He had a starring role in each. But David Evanier, in *Woody: The Biography* (2015), had the highest praise for *Light Bulb*:

> It is his finest play, a great leap from the dreadful *Don't Drink the Water*, and some steps ahead of the charming *Play It Again, Sam*….It was named one of the outstanding plays of the 1981-82 Broadway season and was included in the notable Otis Guernsey's *Best Plays* series.

Light Bulb had a stellar cast including Beatrice Arthur and Danny Aiello, both of whom were already established Broadway actors. Reviewers, however, were most impressed by twenty-four-year-old Brian Backer in his debut Broadway role. Bearing a strong resemblance to Woody Allen, Backer played Paul Pollock, the son of a nagging mother and a philandering father. Set in a small lower-middle-class Canarsie household in 1945, the play reveals the claustrophobia of tenement living. As an escape from the tension and tedium, Paul Pollock has taken up magic as a hobby. He is painfully shy and obviously damaged by his dysfunctional family. He speaks with a severe stammer, making the character simultaneously comical and pitiable.

Backer recalls that he read for the part at least four or five times. During the audition process, director Ulu Grosbard sent him to the Communications Reconstruction Center in Manhattan, which provides therapy for individuals with speech impediments. Backer reviewed hours of videotapes of individuals who stuttered, and found that there was "anguish in the eyes as they were about to stutter," which he found "heartbreaking."

After receiving the part, Backer had a mere three weeks of rehearsal, not only to create the character conceived by Allen, but also to learn several challenging magic tricks. Robert Aberdeen, an actor and a magician who served as the magical director for *Light Bulb*, praised Backer for his dedication to the mastery of the magic effects written into the script. After completing rehearsals with other members of the cast, Backer would spend hours in the evening practicing with billiard balls, decks of cards and, of course, the floating lightbulb. Aberdeen recalls that director Grosbard was extremely demanding of Backer's acting, but seemed to care little whether the secrets of the magic tricks might be exposed to the audience. When asked if Grosbard was a tyrant, Backer empathetically explained, "Ulu Grosbard was under tremendous pressure. After all, Woody Allen had already become a show business luminary. It had to be extremely stressful for Ulu with Allen looking over his shoulder." Backer recalls Allen made no effort to hide his success; he regularly arrived at the theater in his cream-colored Rolls-Royce.

Some of the magic effects in *Light Bulb* would be challenging even for an accomplished magician. For example, the effect of billiard balls that multiply at the magician's fingertips requires extreme dexterity. Playing card flourishes demand endless practice. Both Aberdeen and Backer recall, however, that one of the easiest tricks to perform consistently received the greatest reaction from the audience: in Act I, Paul demonstrates his magical prowess to his father, played by Danny Aiello. He takes his father's tie and cuts off the bottom half, while the top half remains dangling around his father's neck. Paul places all parts of the tie in a special cloth bag. At first Paul's father protests that the tie was very expensive, but then he is genuinely impressed when Paul removes the tie he has fully restored from the bag. Aberdeen remembers that the audience always broke into applause at this moment. Not only was the effect surprising, it was one of the few triumphs Paul had in the entire play.

Aberdeen and Backer remember that Allen made very few appearances during the rehearsals and performances. Backer inevitably had more contact with Allen, but in most cases, Allen didn't speak to him; instead, he would leave notes for Backer in his dressing room that critiqued Backer's performances. Backer and Aberdeen both recall an instance when Allen was present while the play was still in rehearsal. Allen clumsily dropped the loose pages of the script, causing them to scatter on the floor. As he leaned over to pick up the pages now completely out of order, he said, "This may turn out to be the perfect rewrite."

Early in the rehearsal schedule, Backer learned that Allen felt that he was not the right actor for the role. While Allen later acknowledged that his initial assessment was wrong, Backer inevitably felt uncomfortable in Allen's presence. He remembers passing Allen and Mia Farrow walking outside the theater. Rather than nod or say hello, Backer simply looked away. Describing the episode, Backer felt he may have handled the situation badly; to this day, he wonders whether he could have established a greater rapport with Allen if he had stopped to talk at that moment.

Backer found his first Broadway experience overwhelming. He consistently felt he would be fired at any moment. While most of the cast remained somewhat aloof, Backer found Danny Aiello to be kind and supportive. Other members of the cast criticized him freely if they felt he did not pay them proper respect, or if he fumbled some props.

Ultimately, however, it was Backer who received accolades for his role in *Light Bulb*. He received the 1981 Tony Award for Best Performance by a Featured Actor in a Play, the Drama Desk Award for Outstanding Featured Actor in a Play, and the Theater World Award. Backer was stunned by this attention and surprised when people actually waited after the Tony ceremony to get his autograph. Harvey Keitel, John Travolta, Alan Alda and Al Pacino, as well as other prominent actors, came to see his performance after his Tony win. Woody Allen sent him a telegram saying, "Finally, someone who deserves the Tony, got it. P.S. I wish I did look like you." Backer's awards were the reason the play was held over for an additional week.

Light Bulb has been described by some critics as semi-autobiographical; Allen, himself, however, describes it as a satirical parody of Tennessee Williams' *The Glass Menagerie*. In Allen and Bjorkman's book, Allen appears to minimize the significance of the play, "I wrote it for the Lincoln Center just for the fun of it. It was a little idea I had, and I never did anything with it. I just let it be."

If *Light Bulb* is autobiographical, it is more about an artificial persona Woody Allen developed over the years. There is no evidence that Allen ever had a speech impediment, and certainly early in his life, it was apparent to most he was headed for success. David Evanier's *biography* provides this analysis:

[Paul] is clearly not the feisty Woody who surmounted his environment and escaped Brooklyn at such an early age. Allen's childhood friends told me that Allen never had a stammer and was basically in charge of his life from the start. It could be interpreted as the Woody who might have been, or Woody at an earlier stage, or lingering depressive strands of the inner Woody's darker memories of his childhood.

When both Backer and Aberdeen were asked whether they thought Allen is genuinely shy and socially ill at ease, both acknowledged that it was impossible to tell. There can be little doubt, however, that Allen likes his privacy and that he limits his contact with people with whom he works. All his biographers agree that his early stage fright as a stand-up comedian was undoubtedly genuine. Nevertheless, as he became more successful, he made several television appearances. Allen's close friend and fellow magician, Dick Cavett, promoted Allen to several talk show hosts. During his television appearances, Allen presented a plausible confidence as a panel member or a host. Allen is well known as an obsessive workaholic, and it is possible that his distance from other people provides him with greater time and energy to work. In Allen and Bjorkman's book, Allen states, "I'd rather struggle with films than struggle with other things."

Light Bulb featured several standard magical effects that can be purchased at any magic shop: the egg bag, the change bag, and the milk pitcher are classic pieces of magical apparatus. However, the extraordinary illusion in the play is Blackstone Sr.'s floating lightbulb, which is anything but a hobbyist's prop. Currently, it is performed in its entirety by only two magicians, Darren Romeo and Hans Klok, each of whom has a license from the Blackstone estate to do so.

"The floating lightbulb" framed Allen's play, performed at the very beginning of the Act I, and again its closing, but the illusion was not integral to the plot. One cannot help but wonder whether this mesmerizing levitation was added after the first draft of his script. Perhaps, it was inspired by Harry Blackstone Jr.'s performance of the illusion on the Broadway stage just months before the opening of Allen's *The Floating Light Bulb*.

APPENDIX I

Made to Measure Man
A WEISSENBERGER ROMANTIC SUSPENSE NOVEL, BOOK ONE

Garth Matthews, dean of Chicago's newest law school, doesn't see it coming.

And if brilliant Matthews can't see it coming, nobody can.

So it's not looking good.

NATURALLY, MATTHEWS IS THRILLED to receive a multimillion-dollar award for his educational leadership.

But before he knows it, he becomes entangled with the shrewd, gin-guzzling, hysterically funny matriarch of the bestowing European charity—and the intrigue doesn't end there! Clues are mounting that the foundation is really a cover for international art theft and that Matthews is being set up as its prime suspect.

Then—*as if this weren't complicated enough*—Matthews finds himself utterly captivated by Julia, the matriarch's beautiful, enigmatic granddaughter.

Together, Matthews and Julia share quiet evenings at tucked-away restaurants in New York City, fine wines, and warm, wide-ranging intellectual conversation. For the first time since his wife's death, Matthews feels solace and a growing, tender love in his relationship with Julia.

That is, when he isn't trying to unravel the plot spinning around the foundation that may have put his own neck on the line!

And where does Julia fit in?

Could she be his true love–indeed, his soul mate?

Or is she part of the web luring him in with her wiles–possibly even the family's mastermind?

Race through Matthews' ten life-changing days that swirl with false identities, threats of criminal embezzlement, and a building–*possibly dangerous*–passion, days that will change his life forever!

Appendix II

Companions by Contract
A Weissenberger Romantic Suspense Novel, Book Two

It's an unorthodox contract.

And those can prove deadly.

Craig North, the charismatic, wealthy managing partner of a prestigious Chicago law firm, seeks to hire a companion to provide him with platonic, pleasant camaraderie—and, as he repeatedly assures both his colleagues and himself, nothing more.

So he is delighted when the refined and lovely law student Rebecca Bellow applies for the job.

With an executed contract explicitly prohibiting any form of romance between them, Rebecca happily settles into her private, beautiful apartment in North's Georgian mansion, even finding a Mercedes at her disposal.

And as the friendship between employer and companion warms over elegant dinners, animated conversations, and old movies, both think:

"This is just too good to be true!"

And they're right.

Suddenly and inexplicably, Rebecca becomes the target of an international organized crime syndicate.

North–not even an amateur sleuth–leaps in to save her and untangle this deadly mystery, putting his own life on the line. He enlists an eclectic collection of friends to help: Rebecca's racy ex-roommate, a law school student as well-versed in seduction as jurisprudence; a down-on-his-luck private investigator with a penchant for liquor; even a cabal of vengeful of lawyers hatching a conspiracy against North.

As the murderous mob becomes more brazen, Rebecca and North's feelings for one another deepen into a love clearly forbidden by their employment contract.

But soon that becomes the least of their concerns.

Have these "Companions by Contract" entered into the deadliest agreement of their lives?

t

www.ingramcontent.com/pod-product-compliance
Lightning Source LLC
Chambersburg PA
CBHW062046090426
42740CB00016B/3036